C000214386

Take Your Armour

and

Have a Cup of Tea

Angie Northwood

About the Author

Angie Northwood lives and works in beautiful west wales with her husband Rob and their two adult children, Jake and Molly. Together they have created Spirals of Wellbeing, a place of 'peace, creativity and healing'.

Not liking labels, Angie describes her work as a 'basket of womb and soul wisdoms', from which she offers women pathways to awakening and healing using Soulful Facilitation, Soul Realignment readings, Moon Mother Blessings and Healing, Reiki and Holistic Intuitive Massage.

As well as working with individual clients, Angie also holds monthly Dark Moon Circles and World Wide Womb Blessing Circles. She facilitates a monthly online group, Menopause Wisdom.

Take off Your Armour and Have a Cup of Tea is Angie's first book.

Find out more about Angie and her work at

www.spiralsofwellbeing.co.uk

and on Facebook at

Angie Northwood

Soul Wisdom@SoulWisdomwithAngie

 – Soul to Soul and Menopause Wisdom

Foreword

I'm probably not going to read this book. Unusual perhaps for a person writing it's forward to admit such a thing. It may even be of some surprise to hear this for those of you reading it. Part of me was worried about telling my mother this, as wanting to share your achievements with those you love is natural, understandable and innately desirable. I know how much of herself Angie has put into writing this book and how gratifying it must feel to have something you've written published. So, like I said, part of me was worried about telling her I didn't want to read it. But I needn't have been. With a smile and a nod, she said "I completely understand" and that was all that was needed really. But we spoke some more and I told her a lot of what the book covers is too close to home, too personal and besides I lived through it all anyway. Perhaps not from Angie's perspective, but I was there and at least for the time being, I do not need to relive those moments. It was during that conversation I was offered the opportunity to write this forward. "Who better" she said, and with that I knew I had some thinking to do.

How can I put into words my connection to the author and to the story you are about to read? What can I say in regards to the part I played in my mother's experiences? I quickly came to the realisation that words sometimes are simply not enough and that this is one of those times. Regardless, let me say this. My mother's love has been an endless source of support and guidance to me and without it I would not be the person I am today. She has always said that my sense of justice and courage to fight for what I believe in is something she respects and admires about me. It is however; if I can truly claim such a thing, only through example that I have come to possess such qualities. Watching my parents battle with the education system, the medical community and anyone else who stood in the way of my sister being treated fairly, is a large part of why I am who I am.

I could perhaps talk about my mother's strength and how, in the face of insurmountable odds, she battled forth unwavering. But this would not be entirely true. She is strong, one of the strongest people I know, but she's also human and all of us have times where we are vulnerable. Without people around us who are willing to help in these moments it's all too easy to lose one's self and shy away from what you know to be true or right or what must be done. I have a memory from my childhood that has always stuck with me. When I was very little, perhaps only seven or eight I remember waking up to hear my mother on the phone and as I listened, I could hear her crying. I came to realise she was speaking to her mother, my grandmother, about my sister. I was vaguely aware that Molly was not doing some of the things expected of a child her age and that my parents were a little worried about this. But I was assured that it would be ok and that I didn't need to worry myself about it. But as I listened, I began to realise my mother was worried, very worried. I got out of my scaffolding bed and crept past the mural of the Yellow Submarine she had painted for me on my bedroom wall. I opened my door and walked to the stairs just outside my door where the phone lived. I wrapped myself around my mother in what I hope was a comforting hug. It was probably then that I first realised my sister would need more help than usual to get by in the world and that perhaps my parents would too.

I know I'm mentioned in this book and part of me is curious to know how and in what context. For the most part however, I just hope that my mother's story, my family's story can bring some measure of strength to those who need it. Maybe more importantly though, I hope that when you're at your most vulnerable, this book will be there for you to help you when you need it most. One more thing. It would not be right of me if I didn't mention how proud I am of my mother, and my father; Angie and Rob, for being the supportive, loving and nurturing parents that they are.

Thank you guys!

Jake Northwood

Dedicated to all the people who have the courage to be vulnerable as you stir the cauldron of change.

Table of Contents

Preface

In the following pages I have woven the story of being a mother of a disabled child into the story of being a mother who has *gathered her bones*. This is the story of why and how I became an Inclusion Warrior in order to fight for the rights of my child. The story of how over the years of fighting battles, protected by a fierce armour I had unknowingly shielded myself with, I lost touch with my instinctual wisdoms.

This is also the story of finding and remembering my Womb and Soul Wisdom, of doing my inner work to heal the *mother wounds*, heal from my battle wounds and of learning to navigate my menopausal years into the magnificence of becoming Crone.

The two stories are inseparable.

I'll be clear right from the start. Molly is the most wonderfully expressive person I have ever known. She laughs every day, she sings every day, she shouts when she's angry, she cries when she's sad, she's quiet when she needs to be. Molly has not lost touch with her instinctual, intuitive self. She is uncluttered and non-conformist. The beauty of her 'forever innocence' is that she maintains her innate ability to be herself. She has no pretence, no projecting. I know where I am with her, she doesn't disguise or hold back with what she's feeling. This is so refreshing and let's be honest, it's rare to know someone who is fully expressed. I celebrate and rejoice in her ability to teach me and others on so many levels.

It's not always easy; being a mother of a dependent adult child has challenges. Many years ago, a woman said to me

"I bet you wish you had a magic wand" (to change Molly).

I did not wish that then and I do not wish it now. I would not change any aspect of my daughter. I would however change many aspects of how society regards and treats people who appear on the surface to be *'too different'*.

Models of Disability

I have a very specific view on what disability is and what it isn't. I am clear about what I need to challenge and why. I am committed to creating community, planning a positive future for my daughter, so far as I can, for beyond the time that I am here. I cannot do this alone. I need my family, my friends, my community to stand with me, to offer support, to share ideas, to be an active participant in creating inclusive solutions for the inclusion of *all*, in whatever way is right for an individual.

I don't like labels, they are divisive, they pigeon hole people. We have a tendency to define people by their label, reducing a person to one specific aspect of who they are. The label 'Special Needs' is a bugbear for me, it's a perfect example of the negative impact a label has. I have known many parents of disabled children who *do* like it and definitely prefer it to calling their child disabled. The disabled adults I worked with over many years who were activists in the Inclusion Movement, also preferred the term 'Disabled' and like me, objected to the label special needs. So, what is the difference? I'll start by explaining the two models of disability.

Medical Model of Disability.

A disabled person is regarded as '*broken'* or having something '*wrong'* with them that needs to be fixed or mended. If they are fixed enough, they can be included in ordinary mainstream life. If not, they will be segregated/excluded. The disabled person is the problem. The medical model is also steeped in the patriarchy. It's all about control over others, power over others. Absent of empathy or compassion.

Social Model of Disability

A person who is, e.g. a wheelchair user or has learning difficulties is only disabled when physical or attitudinal barriers exclude them from participation and inclusion. When adjustments and differentiation is implemented, they still have their learning difficulties or are a wheelchair user but they are no longer disabled. Societal discrimination is the problem.

Special Needs

In my view, and experience, labelling a person as having special needs somehow sets them outside of community. The term infers a need to be treated differently, delicately or even with caution. My 'disabled' daughter *is* special, and so is my non-disabled son, my husband and me. We are *all* special because we are all human and we all have such amazing potential. As far as *needs* go, I believe we all have the *same* needs (regardless of being disabled or non-disabled). We all have the need to be loved, to belong, to participate, to contribute, to be heard, to be seen, to be valued. We may need to experience these things in slightly or exaggeratedly different ways. Perhaps to be supported by another or others, sometimes frequently, sometimes occasionally, sometimes always. The needs are not special, they are simply what makes each of us human.

And let's not forget, *we are all interdependent – we are all interconnected,* we all need each other, practically, emotionally and spiritually. It's what makes us human.

My hope is that by writing this book and sharing my experiences there will be something that resonates for each person who reads it. I was asked very early on who I wanted my audience to be. "*Everyone*" was my response.

Initially I had thought it would be a book for parents of disabled children, which it most certainly is, because even though I know the way I do it, is not the way every parent will do it, I do know the tools and strategies described are useful for every child and parent.

There-in lies the second group of people I want this book to reach – every parent, and friends of parents, colleagues of parents, teachers, the bloke who works in the supermarket, the woman who runs her own business, politicians, everyone, because we are all in this together, this life, this world.

We have a collective responsibility now more than ever to heal the planet and to heal the planet we need as human beings to heal ourselves. When we heal, we have greater capacity to love, to love ourselves and therefore to love others. A problem to resolve then, is we have all been conditioned in all sorts of ways for so very long and the result is that so many of us are cut off from our feelings. We are not, generally speaking, taught to look out for each other, to offer kindness to those in distress or isolation, to give without needing to receive back, to receive without guilt or shame, to nurture and nourish ourselves in order to nurture and nourish others.

We have been told to be independent, stand on our own two feet, that we don't need others. We have been fooled into thinking that we should always be strong, always be happy, always be busy, always do as we are told because others know better.

We have been taught to fear certain groups of people; historically disabled people are one of those groups.

I was taught about the history of disabled people when I became involved with a group called Parents for Inclusion. It was not an easy story to hear, particularly because I am a parent of a disabled child. If my daughter had been born only one generation before, the reality is that her life would probably have been very different, in the worst possible ways.

Parents and communities were told by those in authority that a '*broken*' child, a child who was different, a child who was therefore '*in valid*', did not belong at home or in their communities. These extreme views still persist, disabled children are still separated from parents, family, home and community. Still shut out of the expansiveness of the world in which they have so much to offer and so much to receive.

It is as true for disabled people as it is for any other minority group, separation, segregation, discrimination and oppression perpetuates a lack of understanding, a lack of experience, a lack of acceptance – these attitudes grow into fear or hate or intolerance because of ignorance.

Bleak isn't it.

Of-course times and attitudes *have* changed and continue to change, but it is so slow! This is 2019 not the dark ages. We see around the world political leaders fooling disaffected people and propping up the elite and in doing so have little or no regard for basic human rights. I know that on the flick of a switch those dark ages could return so easily.

I also know that there is a new paradigm emerging. People *are* awakening, all over the world. People are realising, and children are a strong voice in this, that our planet is beautiful and deserves our love and care.

For all of us who have awakened and feel our deep connection to Earth, a heartfelt connection, there is hope through commitment to living with integrity, acting with kindness, expressing ourselves from an open and loving heart.

This is a reality; this is a future.

Our perception of the world we live in very much depends on what we choose to read, to listen to, to involve ourselves in. If we allow ourselves to be bombarded with the fear mongering of the controlling patriarchy, we will perceive the world as a dangerous, fearful place. Being in a constant state of fear blocks our potential.

When we are able to see the world as a place also full of beauty, we begin to embrace our potential within it, we will no longer buy into the very things which destroy our world and ourselves. The old paradigm of scare mongering from Governments and corporations, keeping the masses in a constant state of fear is crumbling. Our systems have to change.

The shift taking place is empowering more and more people to realise our systems are, generally speaking, failing very many of us. Schools are an example of this. The school system is where the control of our future generations starts. Many schools have sadly become a linear, test obsessed, restrictive, unimaginative and *controlling* environment. It is a system designed to churn out robots into jobs, if your 'lucky' and which are largely meaningless, to prop up the system which keeps the 1% in control – a cycle that has brought us to our knees and disconnected us from our soul and from our heart. I say more about school and the struggles there were to support Molly in a system designed to 'manufacture economic puppets'. A child who will not contribute economically once she becomes an adult is *still* regarded as a '*burden*' in the society we currently live in.

However, in the world that has awakened, the soul connected, open hearted, compassionate world, my daughters' gifts are valid, celebrated and treasured. The labels fall away, I no longer have to say she has learning difficulties, she is disabled, she communicates differently.

She just *is.*

I do use the words disabled, impairment, learning

difficulties in this book because it is the language that most people, at this point in time, understand. As I have been writing this book, I have realised more and more how uncomfortable I feel using this old language. I don't introduce my husband pointing out those things that may be unfamiliar or different to others in order to try and explain who he is. It would be absurd. I feel it is equally absurd to continue to do so for my daughter. To do so continues to model to others that difference needs to be explained. I am at a stage in my life where I have enough wisdom to know I step out of my integrity and do Molly a disservice, each time I introduce her to others saying anything other than "This is Molly"!

I have written this book also because when I am gone, others will be responsible for my daughter. Apart from the everyday, practical stuff those people/persons will need to know about, and which I write about in the following pages, there are other matters that are significantly important to Molly's wellbeing.

In addition to the practical, there is her spiritual, her emotional, her soulful and physical wellbeing. Woven into this story then, is my knowledge and experience of the female life cycle, Molly's menstrual cycle, my menopause experience, healing and transformation.

How Molly is supported, guided, held and nurtured throughout her life cycle will make all the difference to how she experiences the rest of her life *and* to those who are providing for her.

It is, at this time of me writing, still the case that in the mainstream, women's health continues to be treated in much the same way as my mother's generation. I know this from my own experiences and from the women I work with as a healer and Soulful Facilitator.

Sedation of emotional issues, cutting out our wombs as a first option, treating the symptom and not exploring and treating the cause persists in mainstream medicine.

Molly will always have other people making choices on her behalf. I want those people to have access to this book, I will be writing this into my Will and Letter of Wishes so that they understand she does have a voice, a view of what she wants. I intend it to be a reference book for those people and I hope others will find it useful for their own choices in how a loved one, or indeed yourself, will be cared for after they have passed.

I originally had the intention for this book to be *all* about celebrating my daughter, focusing on the gifts she brings to my life and to the world. How much I have learnt from her, how she has shown me ways of being an *Unbound Woman* and a *Wild Woman*. But it would have been unbalanced, lacking Truth and authenticity if I only shared the good, happy, easy, beautiful times.

The reality is that sometimes my heart feels so heavy, the immensity of what it is to be a mother of a disabled child in a world in which the majority has not yet reconnected to love, overwhelms me with the fear I feel for my daughter.

She will always be reliant on others for her care and wellbeing, if love for her does not exist in that, a life becomes hollow and meaningless. Over the last 24 years, I have rarely talked about the difficult stuff. I have felt guilty and disloyal just thinking about it. That if I openly express "*This is so fucking hard, please help me*", I would be betraying my love for her and revealing my own *vulnerability.

The fear and anger I feel in this world, which persists in being closed off to people who are 'different', at times has been paralysing. Let's be honest, if the world was full of love, I wouldn't need to be fearful for my daughter just because she has learning difficulties. And, yes, I do know the world *is* also full of love, there are beautiful, loving, giving people, I know many of these people. What I'm expressing is the polarity of being, the polarity of love and hate, being open and being closed.

When things are good and easy and flowing and beautiful it is great being a parent of a disabled child – because she is no longer disabled, she is simply my child.

When things are bad and difficult and ugly it is *so* difficult being a parent of a disabled child because in this polarity, that is *why* she is disabled. It is not her learning difficulties that disable her, it is disabalism – the discrimination, oppression and lack of support which disable her, and for that matter me!

When we have no support, I have little or no time to focus on my business, my writing, my need for rest and relaxation, relationships other than that with my daughter. In years gone by, I became depressed because of depletion. I became depleted because I gave out too much without receiving back. I paid no attention to my own needs for nurturing and nourishment.

It is these issues too which I write about in the following pages, sharing what I have experienced in relation to unwellness, to healing and finally to transformation.

I write from my perspective as a woman and my focus is primarily on offering the wisdoms I have gathered to other women. But this does not exclude men, the more men who are offered an insight into the female life cycle, the greater is the opportunity for open, honest conversation between us. It becomes an opportunity to break down barriers and taboos and therefore to honour, respect and embrace the beauty of a changing women as she moves through life.

I asked my partner when I became menopausal if he was prepared to walk the path of change with me, I am pleased to say he has and our relationship is so much the richer for it.

So, welcome women and men! I will share with you the dark as well as the light. I am sharing what I have experienced and what I have learnt. There are inclusive tools, strategies, ideas and solutions I have used at various times in Molly's life and my transformation. I continue to learn along with Molly, as she continues to develop her own understanding and place in the world. The gifts my daughter has given me and the gifts I pass on to her are the core of our relationship and the tale I wish to leave behind. Molly will not have children and so will be the last in our matriarchal lineage.

***Wild -** a term used by Clarissa Pinkola Estes in her book Women Who Run With The Wolves – meaning, 'a woman who thunders after injustice, the eyes of intuition, the one we leave home to look for, the one we come home to, she is the life/death/life force…'*

***Unbound** - a term coined by Nicola Humber in her book Unbound, meaning 'a woman living her fullest, freest, most magnificent life'.*

***The mother wound** - wounding created through lack of adequate or good enough mothering. A mother who was not emotionally available to you as a child. The wounding is often a repetition of your mother's own mother wound.*

***Vulnerability -** as defined by Dr Brené Brown, is "uncertainty, risk and emotional exposure." Brené says that "vulnerability is the birthplace of love, belonging, joy, courage, empathy and creativity. I say "Yes to that!"*

***Gathered my bones -** as defined by Clarissa Pinkola Estes in her book Women Who run with The Wolves, meaning a woman who remembers, who has come back to her wild, instinctual self, her wild soul, who does her inner work.*

My Daughter is your Daughter

It has taken great courage over the years to stand up to and challenge the barriers some people have tried to restrict, inhibit or exclude Molly with. It is courageous because the oppression is a powerful force, it is designed to break us and control us and has been around for a very long time.

There is a hidden history in the UK about the treatment of disabled people. Unless you are specifically looking for that history you are unlikely to ever know about it.

This history is shameful and for me, very frightening, it is the stuff of my nightmares. I was dreading writing this piece and I do not want to linger on this subject, but it needs to be here, because, for as long as we, society, accept segregation of disabled children into special schools, adults into institutions, the abuse of adults with Autism and learning difficulties, the

1

exclusion of disabled people through inaccessible provisions and disablist attitudes, for as long as we uphold our shameful past and collude with a shameful present nothing will change.

It is time to open our eyes, to reflect on our own attitudes and beliefs, question what we have been led to believe and challenge what we have been shown.

While I was preparing to write this piece, I had a dream. I work with my dreams and so on waking I recorded it, knowing it would provide me with insight and guidance.

My Dream. I am knocking on the front door of a woman I know. She stays behind the shut door. She has a large, fierce, barking dog beside her. I remain standing in front of the door with my gentle, calm dog. I ask the woman if she is coming out. She says 'no, it's too dangerous'. I say 'oh, that's a shame'.

I interpret the fierce, barking dog as my rage and anger and perceive it to be dangerous. The woman keeping the dog shut up behind the closed door I see as that part of me who feels safer to keep the rage and anger shut up inside. Feeling that it is too dangerous to let the anger and rage out. The gentleness of the dog on the outside (that which is visible to others), along with the simple response of 'oh, that's a shame', symbolises a prompt from myself to allow the fierceness to be expressed, knowing I hold within, a balance of gentleness and fierceness and that it is safe to express the anger and rage.

I first saw images of people with learning difficulties and mental health illness, who had been locked up in asylums and institutions, at a training conference. I also learnt that for hundreds of years, disabled people have been dehumanised, thought to be a burden on society, and a punishment from God.

Under Hitler's Third Reich many thousands of disabled people were experimented on and exterminated in the death camps. Hitler was not though the first to conceive of this idea, in 1908 D.H.Lawrence wrote

'If I had my way, I would build a lethal chamber as big as the Crystal Palace, with a band playing softly, and a Cinematograph working brightly; then I'd go out in the black streets and main streets and bring them all in, the sick, the halt and the maimed; I would lead them gently, and they would smile me a weary thanks; and the band would softly bubble out the 'Hallelujah Chorus'.

Lawrence was not alone in his view that disabled people were of no value, that they had no place in society, and that they should be sterilised - without consent.

It was in the 1900's that, Frederick Galton, the cousin of Charles Darwin, led the Eugenics movement here in the UK. The Eugenics Movement held the view that people with learning, mental health and physical impairments were a '*burden to society*' and a '*danger to our race*'. Within the movement were prominent scientists and politicians from the right and left of politics, including Winston Churchill. Their views were not regarded as offensive, Galton in fact received many awards for his work, including a knighthood.

In 1912 the first British Eugenics Conference was held, at which Churchill attended along with 400 delegates and Charles Darwin's son presided. They lobbied parliament for groups of scientists to search the country to identify the '*unfit*', to have them arrested, and then to segregate those people into special colonies or have them sterilised.

In 1913, local authorities were given permission by the 'Mental Defectives Act', to remove people considered to be '*defective*' from their homes. This included children. Doctors were given the authority to decide what category these people belonged to e.g. Cretin, Moral Defective and Imbecile. These men, women and children were then institutionalised in asylums for life. Their liberty was taken from them. *(Source; Incurably Human by Micheline Mason and The New Statesman).*

As I learnt these terrible truths I wept, I left the conference room, it was too painful and terrifying. Those images and historical facts have stayed with me, tucked away in my mind, impossible to erase once seen and heard.

So, if my daughter had been born here in the UK in the early 1900's she would have been regarded as *'feeble minded', 'vermin',* a *'burden'* and a *'threat'* to our society and race. She would have been institutionalised, probably mistreated and abused in the most horrific ways.

But even worse is the scary truth, that abuse of people with learning disabilities *still* happens. You may recall the BBC Panorama programme in 2011, (a current affairs programme in the UK), which exposed systematic abuse of residents in a home for people with learning difficulties. The Government's response was, that they stated there was no place for these Institutions in today's society and called for them to be closed.

However, eight years on and I heard on the radio today (2019) that another Panorama programme has again exposed systematic abuse of residents who have learning difficulties and Autism. I heard the recording of a woman with Autism screaming with absolute terror as male carers restrained her. The male carers had been deliberately called upon, knowing the woman is frightened of men and that they are a trigger to her distress.

Just take a moment to pause and re read that. This is 2019, in the UK.

If Rob and I died today, the local authority has the power to place Molly somewhere other than her home if they deem that to be in her best interests – possibly in a place as described above.

It took until 2001 for the Special Educational Needs and Disability Act to be brought in, which has paved the way for improvements in education, but we continue to maintain segregated provisions, still try to correct and normalise impairments, still abort foetus's when identified as being disabled. It is a very dangerous thing to be complacent. It is too easy for us to click on the 'sad' or 'angry' emoji when we are appalled by something we read or see and then we just move on to the next thing.

I had a conversation recently with a friend who works with adults who have learning difficulties and who live in residential care. He spoke about how some members of staff in the home shout at the 'service users' and send them to their rooms against their wishes, simply for being who they are. Firstly, I want to say I hate the term 'service users'. To me, it is yet another label which dehumanises individuals. They are PEOPLE, who use a service, refer to them as people! Secondly, it is in the dehumanising that makes it much easier for those who are supposed to be caring for the residents to treat them disrespectfully, unkindly and uncompassionately. My friend also described how many of the care workers spent much of the time on their mobile phones, regarding the needs of the residents as inconvenient. I had to walk away from the conversation in the end, I feel such rage when I hear these stories.

I will not let my daughter end up in a place like that. I will not.

On some days when I feel this rage, I want to take up my Inclusion Warrior cry and go into battle. How is it that as a society we have become so disconnected from ourselves and as a consequence of that, from each other. Why do so many of us spend so much time glued to our phones, to our computers, to our television. Why do we get wasted every weekend and fool ourselves we had a good time? Why do we run from relationships as soon as it starts to get tricky? Why? Because we have become disconnected to our *heart* and *soul*.

We do not hear bird song, we do not feel the air on our skin, we do not see the tree's come into leaf and blossom. We are oppressed by the demands of work, or no work, oppressed into believing we need to consume and consume and consume *'stuff'*, being fooled into thinking the *'stuff'* will bring us happiness.

We are too afraid to feel our pain. Too afraid to listen to the call of our heart and soul, 'heal me'. Too afraid to belong, or to be vulnerable, or to be angry, or to cry, in case of rejection.

I rage because this disconnection has created a world in which many people no longer know how to love. And I despair for my daughter in a world of people who do not know how to love. She is unable to instigate the relationships she longs for, unable to create herself, opportunities for connection or belonging without the willingness, commitment, creativity and *love* from others.

Without that, she would be isolated, lonely, frustrated and trapped.

It takes more than me to do all this. I cannot be all things, all the time to Molly. Nor does she want me to be. She wants *others*, she wants friendship, she wants intimacy. She cannot go out and get this for herself. I cannot alone provide this for her. It takes a village.

But while each of us is caught up in our own world *of "I'm too busy to….", "I need to do what's right for me", "I don't know how", "It's too hard", "I'm not the right person"* and on and on and on, we have become stuck, unable or unwilling to look inward in order to heal.

We are horrified when we read or hear about an elderly or disabled person who has been abused in a home, and then we forget. All of us will become elderly, many of us will need support.

My daughter is your daughter.

We are all one, on this same planet together, with the same needs, desires, problems and fears. I am raging after hearing my friend's story because it is time for us to step up, to do our work, to look inside, to listen, to heal. Once we heal, we know how to love. When we know how to love, we have the capacity to help others who need our help. We all know the terrible things that happen in old people's homes, residential homes, any institutional homes. My worst nightmare is that Molly, or I, or Rob, or Jake end up in such a place. Surely there is a better option? Surely providing help and support to those of us who need help and support for our children, adult children or parents is a kinder more compassionate solution?

I know how important it is to have time and space for myself. I know how important it is for Molly to have relationships and experiences outside the home. I know that as I grow older, I will need more support than I do now.

I have thought long and hard about whether or not I am being over protective. Am I limiting Molly's experiences? Is she missing out on social interaction, do I limit her choices? Will it be more difficult for her when I am gone because I did not send her somewhere other than home while I am still here?

Each time a Personal Assistant has left the job I ask myself these questions. Each time I feel sad or frustrated that she cannot arrange her own social life, I ask myself these questions.

I was triggered to write this after listening to a Woman's Hour piece on Radio 4. A parent of two 'severely disabled' young people was explaining why she was choosing a residential home for them. Both of her children are teenagers, the mother was struggling. She described first of all the positive, wonderful and beautiful attributes of her children and how very much she loves them and then described the challenges and how she had reached utter depletion.

She articulated her fear of when she is gone, saying that if her children's experience of life is only that which they had with her, how terrible it would be for them once she was gone. Her logic led her to the belief that it is better for her children to go into residential care to get used to her not always being there and to have experiences other than those with her.

Her words and her decision stayed with me throughout that day, it triggered my own fears. On this particular day I was also faced with Molly's Personal Assistant resigning from the job. All my anxieties, fears, doubts, anger, sadness, frustration came flooding in. I took myself off to my room and cried. And as I cried, I was able to release myself from a position of feeling paralyzed and overwhelmed, into a place of inner knowing. I was able to sort through what were my projections and shadows from what I know to be true of Molly.

That is, Molly has a good life.

I know I don't get it right all the time for her, I have come to accept, at long last, that she is not *always* going to be happy. I do wonder if she felt a huge pressure from me to be happy all the time over years gone by, before I was able to let go of the need to make her life perfect. She *does* have a life with experiences other than those with me and Rob. She does make her own choices. She does express what she wants and who she wants to spend time with. She has always been included in community.

The gifts she brings to the world have always been valued and celebrated by us and by others.

And it has always needed the support of others to co-create this.

Residential, special provision will never be a choice I make for Molly, it is not a choice she would make for herself. I write more of this in the coming pages.

When I finished writing about the hidden history, I had the following dream. I share this with you to demonstrate how the past and present oppression has shaped my determination to plan for Molly's future after I am gone.

My dream

The world has been taken over by fascist monsters. I am in a large courtyard with many other people, we have been rounded up by the monsters. They are calling out names in pairs to group us. Two women are called, they are excited and happy and express thanks that they are together.

I know I have to get Molly out, that she is in great danger. I lead her away, hoping we will not be caught.

We are in a house; I have a cat in my arms. The cat is terrified and starving. I place it into a box with other cats. There is a blanket and food, I hand feed my cat.

I am sitting with others who have escaped, I am sawing a lid off a large box so that we can hide in it.

A fascist monster has joined the group, he has come to eat our supplies and to terrorise us. He sees Molly and leans in close to her face, breathing on her he says "we will get you".

My interpretation

I actually think this is mostly literal (because I had the dream after writing the above piece).

The fascist monsters represent any Government which strips away the rights of disabled people, whose policies limit and oppress.

The two women symbolise 'hope', they also represent me and Molly.

Being in a house with cats symbolises safety, comfort, connection to heart. Placing the cat in the box and caring for it by hand symbolises the feminine energy's instinctual response to want to take care of and protect.

The final image I see as a reminder of the threat that on the flick of a switch, our lives, our liberty, can be threatened.

It was a bleak dream but one which I do not have very often; and I am unsurprised that my sub conscious played it out in order to process my revisiting of the harsh and brutal history.

A final word on this topic.

I want to specifically honour the young men and women who have Down Syndrome in the public eye and ordinary day to day life, who have been forging a path of inclusion and changing attitudes. In very recent years we have seen and heard their efforts come to fruition. Beautiful young women becoming models, articulate young men making speeches at the United Nations, happy, smiling children representing clothes companies – all in the mainstream. All positive images and messages.

Such a wonderful contrast to the usual *'look at how awful their lives are'.*

It is not often that people with learning difficulties are given a voice, space or time within the mainstream.

So, I applaud, celebrate and value the courage these young women and men have to manifest these changes.

But let's not sit back and think, OK, great, that's sorted then! It is not.

Let's not delude ourselves that the discrimination has gone. It has not.

Pregnant women all over the world are offered a test for Down Syndrome of their baby. They are still offered a termination if Down Syndrome is detected.

People still stare, feel sorry for, point at, laugh at, move away from people who behave or look different.

People still make uninvited comments about how

sad, or how difficult, or how terrible it must be to have a disabled child.

It is time to shift these perceptions.

Time to value, celebrate and welcome difference.

I invite you to take a moment to reflect on your own attitudes and beliefs around disability.

What have your experiences been in relation to disability?

Learnt Attitudes and Beliefs

When I was 3 in 1964, my parents moved to Colchester in Essex. In those days there was still a lot of beautiful countryside just a walk or bus ride away from where we lived and also just an hour's drive into the City, where my dad worked for a shipping company called Schenker's.

I remember flying kites, sunshine, trips to the coast, riding my bike and sitting under a huge 'Conker' tree talking to the fairies.

I also have a memory, from when I was still a small child, looking over our garden fence to talk with another small child. My mum told me to "*come away from the fence*", saying something like "*there's no point in speaking to her.*" The small child next door had Down Syndrome. This was Experience One.

Some years later, as a teenager, I went to a new, large Comprehensive secondary school, Sir Chares Lucas, which had amazing facilities. There was a theatre and a large heated swimming pool, enormous playing fields, for hockey, athletics and football as well as several netball and tennis courts. We had well equipped science labs, foreign language classes, metal and woodwork classrooms, cooking labs, sewing classrooms, art studios. Truly FANTASTIC resources. Oh yes, and there was also a 'Remedial Unit'. This was a 'Unit' for those children who needed additional support with learning, or 'You Nit', as the children were labelled by the rest of the school as we filed pass them when changing lesson rooms. The segregation was not questioned by anyone it seemed. Experience Two.

During my first year at 'Charly Lucas', a boy named Matthew arrived later in the term. He had been in a car accident resulting in both of his legs being amputated. He was a wheel chair user, and the school was not equipped with disabled toilets or ramps. There were so many staircases linking each floor to each of the many buildings. I remember seeing Matthew struggling up the stairs every day and between each lesson. Matthew had a best friend, Adrian, but not any others as far as I knew. Although I do recall reluctantly going to one of his birthday parties. I also recall our interest in seeing his body when we had a swimming lesson. He was an incredibly strong

18

swimmer and appeared so confident. Experience Three.

I was aware at this time too of a 'strange' yellow bus that drove unseen children to an unseen school in an unseen part of town. Experience Four.

And then there was my Aunty Hilary. Not a real Aunty, but the best friend of my mum and I adored her. Our two families were friends for years. Charly Lucas was just around the corner from where she lived and I often went to visit her at lunch times with my best mates Theresa and Dawn.

I remember on one visit that she was furious. She told us she had been shopping and as she was walking from one shop to another she spotted in the reflection of the windows, a boy behind her. He was mimicking her walk and calling her a 'cripple' and laughing at her. Aunty Hilary, like my mum, had chronic arthritis. She also had one leg shorter than the other and wore a raised shoe. Aunty Hilary was so very upset, she didn't usually express anger or hurt and always put on a 'brave face' with the pain she suffered. But on this occasion, she did not hide her feelings. Experience Five.

My Mother

My mother gave me the best map that she had to help me navigate my life until I began creating my own Paths; and for that I am deeply grateful. When I was a small child, she taught me many beautiful, Soulful things; to hear birdsong, to see the colour of flowers, to smell their scent, to lie on my back and look up into the sky to watch the drifting clouds or the swooping swallows. She taught me to read and gave me books to feed my appetite for adventure and fantasy. She taught me that it was OK to want to climb trees and rub dirt and berry juice on my face.

But when I arrived at the threshold of adolescence her experience had run out. Her map had pieces missing, large pieces and the Paths were no longer clear or inviting, they no longer felt safe to me or to her.

My mother was born at Poppleton Rd, Leytonstone in London on May 8th 1936, the second child of Jane and Norman Smith. Her brother Michael was seven years older, and they were close as they grew up together.

When war broke out in 1939, my mum and her brother were evacuated to Oswestry in Wales. I know their mother and father were there sometimes as there are family photos. Mostly though they were not. Norman Smith was a photographic journalist and he was posted to Africa as a war photographer, he later received an MBE for his services to the country during the war. My mother's mother was ill with angina and died very young when my mum was only 13 years old. Mum's brother Michael had emigrated to Australia when he was 21 years old, he was killed in a road accident by a drunk driver shortly after arriving there. There was a period of time when my mum was cared for by her Aunty Aida, an elderly woman who was Victorian in attitude, and then mum was sent to a boarding school, which she hated and she often inferred she was not treated well there. Mum also told me on two occasions, once when I was still living at home and once when I as an adult with my own family, that during her evacuation she *'had been interfered with by the farmer'*. She never elaborated on this and I did not ask.

Mum's father remarried her mother's half-sister, Eira Jones from Merthyr Tydfil. I have no recollection of my grandfather Norman as he died when I was very young, but I know my mum loved him deeply and they had a good relationship.

My mum met my dad in their early 20's and they

married in 1957, my brother Mike was born in 1958. I followed soon after in 1961 and my second brother, Anthony, in 1964. Dad was employed by a freight forwarding company and was working his way 'up the ladder'. Before Anthony was born, we lived in Ealing in West London in a small flat. My parents did not have a lot of money in those days and mum would often go without a proper meal so that Mike and I were fed well. She would also tell us to be quiet and hide with us until the milkman had gone away from the front door because there wasn't enough cash to pay him. In 1963 we moved to Colchester in Essex to a small maisonette.

When my brother Anthony was a toddler, I have my first memories of my mum experiencing difficult health issues. She had had meningitis as a child and again when we were toddlers, she was, of course, admitted to hospital. My dad had to keep working, so my brothers and I were cared for by a neighbour. I felt abandoned, angry with my mum and resentful of the woman 'pretending' to be my mum. She wanted to hold my hand to cross the road to go the post office. I pulled my hand away in fury and was promptly told off by her and then punished by my dad for being 'naughty', I was told how ungrateful my behaviour was.

That experience remained deeply embedded in my psyche for years, the feeling of abandonment has been a big piece of shadow work for me and continues to catch me out from time to time, particularly in relation to Molly.

A little while after this we moved to one of the modern terraced houses just 3 minutes from the maisonette. This was St Edmunds Court. I liked living there. We had lovely neighbours who had children the same ages as me and my brothers. We would all play together in the gardens or by the garages, driving Mrs Flowerdew mad by throwing our ball up against her wall or over her garden fence again for the fourth or fifth time that day.

St Edmunds Court is where we met Aunty Hilary and her family. Aunty Hilary had a wildness about her, I felt a sense of adventure and freedom in her company. I was able to talk with her as a teenager in a way I was never able or willing to talk to my mum. Aunty Hilary smoked and drank which I thought was exotic and daring, neither of which my mum did.

One summer afternoon mum, Aunty Hilary and Pat (another neighbour) were all sitting under a huge conker tree while we kids were all playing contentedly. I remember observing these three women together, in a world I did not yet understand. My mum was wearing lipstick and was smiling and laughing, she looked so beautiful, so happy, she was something other than what I knew.

We spent a lot of time outside as children. My best memories are of summer days, just sitting and being in nature, making daisy chains or perfume out of flower petals. I liked time alone as much as time in company. I was adventurous too. Long bike rides into the country side on my own or with a best friend was absolute bliss.

Children and adult social time were separate for us. If mum and dad had company, we would be ushered off to our bedrooms. Or if we were to join the company for a meal we had to be well presented and be on our best behaviour. It wasn't like that at Aunty Hilary's house though, there we would have noisy, messy tea times.

In 1967 Dad was by now making enough money to buy their first home. It was across town on a new, modern housing estate. We lived in a cul de sac called Edison Gdns. For the first time, I had my own bedroom, it was a box room really, but I loved it. We also had a small front and back garden, a telephone, with a party line, and a car – registration number KMH 221K. There were lots of children in the cul de sac, we all played outside together and, in each other's houses, a normal suburban life.

On the surface I imagine our family life looked all well and good. In reality my mum was depressed. Dad worked long hours travelling to and from London each day as well as business trips away. He would bring back exotic presents, pistachio nuts, real Turkish Delight, an ornate brass table on wooden legs, a silver wedding belt and copper tea pots from the Middle East. My favourite though of all the gifts he bought mum, was a large bottle of Channel No5, I thought it was the best thing ever. The business trips were amazing experiences for my dad (although he said he hated going there) but for mum less so.

She had three young children, worked part time, ran the home and I am sure was experiencing her own feelings of abandonment triggered by dad's absence. She had never received any support or counselling for her losses as a child, the loss of her family and home when evacuated, the loss of her mother at a young age, the loss of her brother shortly after, the loss of her father at 21. And I have no idea if she ever disclosed to an adult her abuse as a child when evacuated, or if she ever sort healing for that particular wounding.

Like so many women of her generation she was given anti-depressants to push her emotions down into the shadows.

I have always considered my childhood as normal. I wasn't consciously aware of my mother being absent through her addiction to anti-depressants until I was an adult and having counselling myself.

So, for all the moments of nurturing I remember and hold dearly in my heart and Soul, I also remember the wounding. Mums behaviour was erratic and unpredictable when she was taking Valium.

One early evening she asked my brothers and me if we had tidied our bedrooms. I was honest, something we had been taught to be, and said *"No". "Don't you have any consideration for me or your father?"* she shouted at me. I didn't know what 'consideration' meant and so I replied once again *"No".* She grabbed my hand, flew down the stairs with me in tow, put me over her knees and spanked me. We weren't often hit, the occasional slap round the back of the legs (sadly in the 1970's this was regarded as a valid punishment for a 'disobedient' or 'naughty' child) so this physical punishment was utterly bewildering and shocking to me.

I felt ashamed, not good enough and unworthy of my mother's love.

When my dad got home, I was still feeling so sad and confused. When Mum told him what had happened, I hoped in my heart he would scoop me up and tell me it was all OK. I wrapped my arms around his legs and he *said "It's no good looking for sympathy from me, you're to do as your Mother tells you".*

In that moment, I learnt it was not safe to show my vulnerability or express my need for reassurance and comfort. The second shadow piece that has played out in my life for years.

There was a second time my mum hit me. I was about 11 or 12 years old by this point. I have no idea what I had or hadn't done, but whatever it was she was enraged by it. We were stood at the top of the stairs, her screaming something at me and then she lashed out and slapped me hard across my face. She fainted and fell to the floor. I was terrified she'd had a heart attack or something and I rushed over to a neighbour's house for help. She didn't remember hitting me and was clearly shaken, as was I.

Things got worse between us. She had no idea how to mother me during my teenage years. I think she was probably also peri menopausal and for her generation the attitude was to get on with it, not make a fuss, take drugs to dull the whole experience. So, on top of her Valium addiction, because by now that's what it was, she was fighting a huge battle with herself and with me.

I had started menstruating and had my own emotions to deal with. What I was taught about periods was this.

There was a paper bag full of Dr Martin sanitary towels, a sanitary belt and pants hidden away in a drawer for when 'the time come's'. I knew at some point I would start bleeding each month, my mum referred to this as *'The Curse'*.

Most of my peer group at school started bleeding long before me, they had breasts and wore bra's and had an energy about them that alluded me until I was 13 and started to bleed.

I was sat on the loo and noticed there was blood on the toilet paper. I froze. There was a part of me, an ancient part of me, the part of me that remembered my *wild wise self*, and I felt held, just for a moment, barely aware of the feeling, then I was back on the loo, the voices of my brothers, my father and my grandfather all talking in the room below me.

I put a wadge of toilet paper in my pants and went to get my mum. It was all very hush hush; she was practical and got the paper bag from the drawer. The only words I remember her saying over the coming months were something like *"You'll have to be careful of boys now. You don't want them having their evil way with you"*.

Sex education at my secondary school was pretty much of the same attitude. We, the girls, received our lesson, there was only one, separately from the boys, who tried to peer in through the hall windows which had been shielded with curtains. Such was the tension that one girl passed out. This was 1975!

So, there it was, I had transitioned from girl to woman with a message that it is shameful and dangerous being a woman– *'The Curse', "be careful of boys"* – *"have their evil way"*. No celebration and no acknowledgement of the *sacredness, the power, the mystery* that there is in transition from girl to woman.

There were no conversations about how I would feel emotionally different throughout my cycle, sometimes creative, sometimes reflective, sometimes full of energy, sometimes tired, sometimes angry, sometimes dreamy. I wasn't told about these treasures of wisdom because my mother had never been given these treasures, nor her mother before her.

This is where my mothers' map was ripped, this was where the missing piece should have been. I believed my mother's story, that bleeding was a *'Curse'*, that I should keep it hidden, that I had to just put up with the pain when my blood came and that I should learn to control my emotions before my time to bleed if I wanted to avoid being called 'moody', 'hysterical', Balshy', 'drama queen'....... I learnt at school that it was *'just boys being boys'* when they laughed at our 'Jam Rags' and called us bitches if we lost our temper from the relentless teasing. And there were some girls who ridiculed you for not yet using Tampons.

At the time I got on with it, it was just how things were, it didn't really affect me, did it? I mean it's not like I was traumatised or depressed by it, I didn't lose sleep over it. The thing is, unbeknown to me I *was* affected by these attitudes and behaviours, deeply affected. These experiences shaped a view of myself that diminished me as a woman, that drew me away from my innate feminine power, my intuition, my instinct, my *Womb Wisdom*, my instinctual *Wild Woman*.

Molly's experience of her menarche was very different. Although at the time, I had not yet started consciously working with my womb wisdom, I was aware enough that I consciously supported Molly and celebrated her transition. I had been unnecessarily worried about how she would respond to bleeding each month, Molly took it all in her stride.

My mum had poor health for most of her life. She suffered from Rheumatoid Arthritis from her early 30's and was prescribed pharmaceutical drugs for the inflammation and pain. She was on various drugs for the remainder of her life. In her late 30's she had a Hysterectomy and once again was instructed to just get on with it. For every wounding she experienced, she just had to 'get on with it', and this was passed on to me.

Mum managed to wean herself off the Valium eventually, alone and no support, but in later life, when she was in constant and chronic pain from her layers of illnesses, she became depressed again. She resisted taking anti-depressants for as long as she could, but, without any other support being offered she did return to taking them.

It is never too late to connect to our womb and our sacred feminine energy.

I found looking back at my menarche a powerful healing medicine and a potent awakening to the

31

magic of our cyclical nature as women.

Do you remember your first bleed?

How did you feel when you started menstruating?

What were you told about menstruation and becoming a woman?

You may like to record your thoughts and memories in a journal, perhaps have a conversation with a best friend and share your story's together.

Love at First Sight

In 1979 I left home to go to drama school in London. My three years at Mountview Theatre School in North London were brilliant and challenging and formative. Although I did very little acting after I left, the skills I learnt there have stood me in good stead over many years.

In my last year at drama school I fell in love with a boy in my year and we moved in together after leaving Mountview. A little over a year later I became pregnant. It was not planned and not wanted. As soon as I did the pregnancy test and found it to be positive, we both panicked. I phoned our local GP in floods of tears, she said we could come straight over to see her, which we did. She examined me and checked my dates and confirmed I was indeed pregnant. She asked me what I wanted to do. I said I wanted an abortion. She made a referral and at 9 weeks pregnant my boyfriend drove me to a hospital somewhere in north London for a termination.

I was so scared. I remember sitting on the edge of the bed in a hospital gown sobbing and shaking. The nurse was very kind, she sat next to me and held my hand saying *"you don't have to go through with this if you don't want to".*

It was the first time anyone had said this. There had been no offer of counselling, no time or space offered to us to talk about any sort of option.

I am and always have been completely in favour of a woman's right to choose. Having the abortion was the right decision. But. Choosing to have an abortion, not being given any support before or after leaves a wound. I know now that it was at this point, I completely disconnected from my womb, I was 22 years old.

My boyfriend and I struggled on for another year or so before splitting up. I was like a bird who had flown her cage and was content enough to be single.

In fact, I was feeling fabulous! I was working backstage at Cat's (a West End musical theatre show by Andrew Lloyd Weber) as a dresser and on a stall in Covent Gdn Market and so was making enough money to live in a great flat in Battersea and enjoying going out, buying clothes, partying, with responsibility only to myself and my cat Amber, I was feeling very free.

One Saturday night at Cat's, as we were finishing our work up in Wardrobe a friend asked me *"Are you going to Duncan's party tomorrow night?"*

I said *"no"* I wasn't planning to.

"Oh no. You ARE going to Duncan's party tomorrow" my friend replied.

"Why?" I asked

"He's only having it so you can meet a guy he thinks you'll like" she smiled

"Ugh, then I'm definitely NOT going" I answered and set off for home.

Sunday evening came and I felt at a loose end, I asked my flat mate if she fancied going to a party in Camden. Off we went across London to a fantastic squat where my good friend Duncan lived. Duncan had gone to Mountview Theatre School too where we became good friends, sharing a flat along the way and we'd kept in touch since leaving drama school.

Duncan opened the door and grinned broadly seeing me there.

"Darling! There's a gorgeous man in an orange boiler suit sitting in a chair in the corner, you'll love him, his name is Rob!" Duncan declared theatrically.

"Oh, fuck off Duncan, I'm not interested" I smiled.

I made my way into the front room and there he was, just as Duncan had described and I suddenly felt nervous and shy! He *was* gorgeous. I went and sat on the floor with some other people and could feel him looking at me.

Eventually he plucked up the courage to come and sit with me and we started chatting. We chatted all night, we laughed, got very stoned and were both so excited we had met each other. Every so often one or the other of us would go to the kitchen for a drink or something to eat, just an excuse to tell Duncan how wonderful the other was!

"Well, what do you think?" asked Duncan

"Yeah, he's lovely!" I said

"I knew you'd like each other" he said as he hugged me.

And that was it. We fell in love.

Duncan and Rob had been in the revival of West Side Story in the west end. They too had become friends. Like me, Rob had recently split up from a relationship. Duncan had shown him my photo and said he thought we would get on. Rob said he was up for it and Duncan arranged the party just so we would meet. I thank Duncan so much for acting on his intuition. Sadly, he was one of the many who contracted HIV in the early 80's and he passed in 1990, four years after the party.

Becoming a Mother

In 1986 I became pregnant again, this time I was overjoyed. Rob was 21 years old; I was 24. We had only known each other for just over year! But we were madly in love and embraced our new, unexpected situation. My pregnancy was wonderful. I felt so healthy and vibrant and in retrospect I would say I felt like a Goddess.

We planned for a natural birth, in hospital. At that time community midwifes were funded and we had the loveliest group close to where we lived. I enjoyed my visits with the midwives, I felt special and excited and everything was going smoothly. I made up a tape recording of my favourite gentle pieces of music that I played to my baby in my womb and intended to play during my labour. I took Yoga classes and ate a healthy diet; I took good care of myself and my baby.

I had given up work as a dresser at Cat's when I was about 6 months pregnant but I continued to work on the stall in Covent Gdn Market until later in the pregnancy. I recall seeing an adult with Down Syndrome walking past my stall one day and I very consciously pushed all thoughts of disability out of my head. Rob and I attended National Childbirth Trust classes and the only things they never talked about was having a disabled child and a contraption called a Venteuse.

On June 4th 1987 I went into labour.

An ambulance came and collected Rob and I to go off to hospital. It was a LONG labour, 22 hours. The yoga I had done was really beneficial and helped me to stay focused, calm, breath and relax. However, as I got the urge to push things started to go wrong. The midwife was concerned about my baby's heart rate and after allowing me to try pushing for an hour or so she called in the Consultant.

Suddenly the room was full of people. The bright lights were turned on and I was instructed to lay on the table and put my legs in the stirrups. A bag full of metal instruments was tipped out onto a trolley, clattering as they landed. I had no idea what these instruments were. I was given an Epidural, injections into my vagina and was cut. The Epidural did not work, and as a suction cap was placed onto my baby's head, the consultant put his foot on the bed grasping the metal chain attached to a pump, a nurse pumped the air machine beside the bed. I was told to put my chin on my chest and push with all my strength during the next contraction.

My baby was suctioned out and whisked away to be checked and cleaned. The room emptied and Rob looked around aghast at the amount of blood, remarking it looked like World War 3 had taken place. I felt battered and overwhelmed but my baby boy was placed on my chest and I was totally in love. His little head was bruised and elongated by the suction. He took to breast feeding almost straight away and we were taken off to a bed in a ward. He was taken from me again 'so that I could get some rest' and then brought back when he needed feeding. I didn't want him to be taken away, so he was then put in a crib by my bed.

I quickly discovered I had ripped all the muscles in my neck with that final push. The hospital was freaking out that the Epidural had caused some sort of spinal damage and I was given a neck brace to use and not allowed to leave until I got movement back in my neck.

So, there I was, in pain from top to bottom, well from neck to yoni to be more precise, not being

41

able to move but in awe of this beautiful, wondrous little being in my arms feeding from my breasts. He was the centre of my universe.

I stayed in hospital for 5 days before they let me go. I was still in pain but determined to get home where I instinctively knew I would heal better and more quickly.

I loved being a mum. Rob and I adapted well to being parents. We were the first of our peer group to have a baby, my parents were in Colchester and Rob's parents weren't that interested in being Grandparents at that point. So, we pretty much did it all ourselves.

Our relationship changed of course, we had only known each other for a very short time before becoming parents but we found our way of being and it was generally good. Neither of us though wanted to have another baby. We loved Jake so much and couldn't imagine being able to love another child. Nor did we want to have the responsibility of another baby. We missed each other and the lack of time we had together.

In 1993, six years later, Rob had been in Starlight Express (a West End musical) for 6 years and we were feeling trapped, we wanted to break free, do something different. We decided that Rob would leave Starlight Express and we would buy a VW van and do a bit of travelling in Europe. We had some notion that we'd find a cool community we would choose to stay and live in. It was a seed of a dream that took many years to propagate!

We had a fantastic time over 7 weeks in the summer of 1993. Jake was six years old, to share our travelling experiences together as a family was one of the best choices we have ever made.

I think my favourite memory was an evening in France when we all snuggled into the back of the VW with the doors open and gazed up at the sky waiting for a meteor shower. We heard owls hooting and the river rushing by, the humid warm air keeping us alert to the mossies. We waited for what seemed like hours until, we all fell asleep, content and completely in love with the freedom we were experiencing.

The seed of a dream was not the only one planted that summer. Our second child was conceived, planned, and by the time we returned home to London I was already feeling pregnant.

My second pregnancy was not so free flowing as my first. On return to London Rob and I were of course faced with the reality of needing to make money to pay the mortgage and bills, we had to sell our beloved VW, the symbol of our one little bit of freedom. Rob returned to working at Starlight and I continued with my part time job at Jake's school as a learning support assistant and drama teacher.

Rob and I were not getting along. He was not entirely happy with me being pregnant again. It had been me who wanted a second child and he really *'just went along with it'*.

We had been like two ships passing in the night for years while he was in Starlight. He had a show every evening from Monday through to Saturday with 2 shows on a Tuesday and 2 on a Saturday. During the day he more often than not had rehearsal's from 10am all day until the evening show. He was also at this time studying to be a Fitness Instructor. He worked long hours and so had little energy left for me. I was working long hours too as a full-time mother and part time classroom assistant and little energy left for Rob.

The dissatisfaction between us was unspoken. Neither of us dared to address the sadness we were feeling, the fear we no longer loved each other. So, we plodded along, getting on with life and waiting for our baby to be born.

The pattern of behaviour Rob and I chose over

many years from this point was to distract ourselves from the discomfort we both felt. We became experts at pretending everything was fine not only to ourselves and each other but to our families and friends too. We were always perceived by others as the 'perfect couple', in love, happy. And we were those things, *but not always* and when we did experience problems it felt really difficult to tell others because of that perception and I later discovered, asking for help changed the dynamics of some friendships which then did not survive.

The due date for our baby came and went and after a week overdue I was required by the hospital to go in for daily monitoring. What a drag that was.

We were living in Battersea and the hospital was in Tooting, 2 bus rides away. So, every day for 2 weeks, after dropping Jake off to school (I had stopped working by this point) I'd make the long trek over to St George's Hospital. My baby's heart rate was monitored and I had the usual blood pressure test. It was exhausting and felt intrusive into the natural rhythm of pregnancy. Annie, a dear friend at the time, who had agreed to take us to hospital when I went into labour and would be there for the birth, managed to get over from her home in North London to sit with me during one visit.

As we were chatting a young doctor strode into the room, looked at the monitor and started pulling the monitoring equipment off me, saying angrily *"This is a waste of time, I don't know why you're here"* and told me not to keep coming in. Then he just as angrily strode off again. I felt confused, fearful and suddenly abandoned (there was that trigger!).

Ironically, the evening of the next day I went into labour. I hadn't been sleeping much for several weeks as I was by this time 3 weeks over due, huge and uncomfortable. At around just before 3am I felt a whopping contraction. I nudged Rob, who slowly woke from a deep sleep, and said *"it's started"*.

He went to call Jake's best friends mum, Denise, who had agreed to come and fetch him when needed. Then Rob called Annie, who would have to drive from North London to us in South London. She told Rob *"I'll just have a quick cup of tea and be right over"*. Fortunately, he managed to convince her that there really was no time for tea, things were happening very quickly. While we waited for Denise to arrive, Jake was gently rubbing my back, trying to ease the pain as I groaned.

The contractions were rolling like thunder, no gaps and phenomenally intense!

Denise arrived and Jake, probably a little shell shocked, went off to his friend's house. At that time in the morning even London roads are clear and Annie arrived after not too long a wait. I was on all fours in the back of her little car, bum squished against the window, howling with a primal urge to push already.

At the hospital, Annie went to park the car and Rob helped me into a wheelchair we found at the entrance of the maternity wing. We were laughing between the moaning and the chair bouncing off the walls as he tried to push it in a straight line.

The midwife on duty was asleep behind the desk and on waking wasn't very enthusiastic about our arrival nor was she convinced when I said I was ready to push. We were taken into a horrible, grey, unwelcoming room as everything else was full, none of the lovely maternity suits we had been shown around on our previous visit was available – it was a busy night. Rob asked for a bean bag, explaining I wanted to be able to move around and use the beanbag to be in a position I felt comfortable in. The midwife, slowly shuffled out of the room, muttering to herself and then about 5 minutes later, slowly shuffled back into our room, dragging the beanbag behind her and unceremoniously dumped it on the floor.

Before she allowed me to get down on all fours, she insisted she do an internal examination. She actually wanted me to get up onto the bed, as this was easier for her but Rob and I insisted that I stay on the floor. She grudgingly did the examination and it was extremely painful. Fortunately, at that point our community midwife arrived and a completely different atmosphere was instantly generated. I was ready to push! And push I did! This was such a contrast to my first birthing. I could feel the power of being a woman, I felt invincible, primal, like a Goddess and the sounds emanating from my deepest being were magnificent.

The baby's cord was around the neck, but our midwife managed to unravel it with no intervention and at 6.30 am our beautiful little girl was born, 3 hours after I went into labour.

The sun was streaming through the window and we couldn't have been happier. A couple of hours later we were back at home and introducing Jake to his sister Molly Moonbeam Sunrise Northwood.

When I had my children, I was not aware of ritual or ceremony for women after we have given birth. I just got on with being a mum and gave no space or time to heal from the physical experience and no conscious thought to the phenomenal transition it is becoming a mother. So, I am sharing the following meditation, which can be done at any time in our female life cycle.

Focusing on our womb and yoni energy helps us to connect to our deepest intuitive and instinctual self.

Our womb (whether you have a physical womb or not) is our creative centre, through which we can create a child, create a home, create our dreams and visions, create the work we truly want to do in the world.

Our yoni is our sacred space of pleasure and desire.

Through focus, we awaken and deepen our connection to our womb and yoni wisdom, we honour the sacred feminine, empowering us to be our most authentic self.

Try doing this meditation at different times in your menstrual cycle or the moon's cycle. You may find it interesting and enlightening to see how your mind, body and spirit respond during these various times.

Womb, Yoni Meditation

Find a quiet, safe, comfortable space, perhaps light a candle and play some gentle music.

Lay down on some cushions or cosy rugs and let your body begin to relax.

When you are ready, bring your attention to your breath and slowly let it deepen and slow.

Continue to breath slowly and deeply, and now, all the way down into your womb, all the way down into your yoni.

Pause

Now, still breathing deeply and slowly, gently lay your hands over your womb centre.

Feel your breath flow all the way down to fill your womb and yoni.

Continue to do this for several minutes.

Observe what arises for you

Long Pause

Moving your hands to your heart, let your breath now fill your heart space.

Observe what arises for you.

Long Pause

Finally, let your arms and hands lay gently by your side and take 3 final deep breaths, exhaling with a sigh or sound.

Let your breathing return to your normal rhythm and pace.

Wiggle your toes and fingers

Have a yawn and a stretch and open your eyes.

Note down in your journal what you experienced.

The Early Years

'Molly is a Moonbeam
And she came from outer space
Molly is a Moonbeam
There's a smile upon her face
Molly is a Moonbeam
And she's shining bright and clear
Molly is a Moonbeam
And we're very glad she's here'
Written by Wendy as a gift when Molly was born.

When Molly was 8 months old my mum plucked up the courage to comment on the fact that she was not developing in the way you would expect. She was right. To be honest, I knew there was something. I took Molly to my GP for the routine check-up babies have at a few weeks old. The GP did the startle reflex test, when they hold your baby upside down for a moment, the baby usually instinctively throws their arms out to break a fall. Molly didn't. The GP did it twice, and twice Molly made no reaction. The GP said *"Oh, not to worry, she probably wants to"*. I did worry though.

My first encounter with what I came to know as

the Medical Model of Disability was at an appointment with a Consultant Paediatrician. I felt no empathy or sensitivity to my vulnerability from him. He told me it was really too early to know what was *'wrong'*. I asked could it be Cerebral Palsy (this and Down Syndrome were the only 2 disabilities I knew). He smiled at this and said "*No. Children with Cerebral Palsy tend to be intelligent*".

By implication he was saying my child would not be intelligent. I left that appointment feeling so lost.

We were at this time moving from Battersea in the borough of Wandsworth to Brixton, which is in Lambeth. Molly was referred to the Early Year's Services there. At about a year old I went to The Mary Sheridan Centre to meet another Paediatric Consultant named Jane Walters. What a revelation she was. On this occasion I did not have to sit opposite the Consultant with a table between us. We were in a comfortable, warm, welcoming playroom. She sat on the floor with me and Molly. She played with her, chatted with me and remarked how very beautiful Molly is. After a while of more play and conversation she told me she thought Molly has Global Developmental Delay and Hypotonia.

In that moment I felt a great sense of relief, I had been told what I was '*dealing*' with.

However, it became apparent to me over time that the label meant nothing in relation to who my child is, it was, just a label.

As the months passed and I became overwhelmed with referrals for Molly to various health and educational professionals I began to lose touch with my innate wisdom of being a mum.

I was sent off to a special school for a mum and baby swimming session specifically for mum's who had a child who was different. I felt instinctively that this separation was unnatural, I was being pushed into a corner and my heckles were beginning to rise.

I remember very clearly walking home with one of the other mothers after a session. She was very animated, talking about her child and how she felt. I was suddenly confronted by her deep-set fear of the attitudes toward disability in her community - *"I will kill anyone who tries to harm my baby"* she said. I hadn't considered the possibility of another human harming a baby because she/he was disabled.

Comments and attitudes were beginning to rear

their ugly heads. *"At least she's pretty"* was a classic*, "I bet you wish you could wave a magic wand?"*, referring to changing her into a *'normal'* baby*, "The gap will get bigger and bigger"* a friend remarked. *"What's wrong with her?" "What's her condition?"*

Each comment, each moment of having other people's beliefs and fears projected toward me and my baby girl was so very painful. Added to which, I had the experiences of disability I had grown up with, which were unconsciously deeply embedded in my psyche.

Once a week a woman from the Early Year's services came to the house to teach me how to play with Molly. At the time I felt that, on the one hand I was being held and supported but on the other it felt completely absurd and unnatural – I knew how to play with my baby, I'd already done it with my son!

There was also a physiotherapist who came fortnightly to show me exercises I could do to help Molly with sitting up and learning to walk. I was given tick charts to monitor her 'progress', which I gave so much focus to I continued to lose, bit by bit, my mother instinct and connection to my own wisdom.

I had tried going out to mainstream play sessions before we moved to Brixton. At that point I wasn't receiving any support nor had a diagnosis for Molly and so was not being signposted or guided to specialist services.

And to be honest those experiences were also deeply painful. I remember watching the other babies and toddlers doing what they do at their various stages of development, seeing the joy on their mother's faces.

I could sense mother's looking at Molly and me and their brains working overtime to try and work out what was going on, and then a comment came at me! A mother sat next to me, she looked at Molly and asked "*How* old is she?". It was such a loaded question, I fought back my tears and bewilderment. I felt like I didn't belong there.

Why did I feel like this? I loved my baby, she was perfect – so why was my heart aching so much?

I felt terribly alone, I did not have a tribe, I had no one with whom I could express my fear, my feelings of vulnerability, no one to hold me and let me cry the tears I needed to cry. I wanted to scream and shout and swear and throw things. But these were not things I had ever been told were OK to do. 'Just get on with it', be strong, smile, tell everyone "I'm fine", was the model I had learnt.

Rob and I were unable to share our feelings, both of us wanting the other to take control, which I did, to deal with the intrusion from specialist services, deal with the looks and comments, deal with the loss of our closeness.

On more than one occasion I was told I was grieving for the loss of the baby I didn't have. I wasn't. I find it extraordinary now that people thought that it was OK to say that, that they thought they were being supportive by giving me a reason for my tears. Telling me I was grieving because my beautiful daughter was not what I had expected! *"F**K OFF"* is what I would like to have said, but I was far too polite for that. The grief I felt was for the loss of my intuition and instinct, for the separation from my *wild, wise self*, from loss of belonging by being pushed toward a segregated life. Through that loss I became lost, adrift, life felt threatening because I was in battle with society's beliefs and attitudes which I knew were damaging and my only resolve at that time was to wear a suit of armour and stand firmly in my masculine energy.

In many situations asserting my masculine energy served me well and so I became very attached to it, believing it was the only way to survive. Over the years though, I lost touch with my feminine self, my energy was unbalanced. I forgot to take care of myself. I felt oppressed.

On Molly's 1ˢᵗ birthday it was a beautifully hot, sunny day. Jake was at school and Rob at work. I took a blanket out into the back garden and gathered Molly's toys and presents. I sat Molly on the blanket, propped up by cushions to prevent her toppling over. She was content and smiling, so beautiful. My eyes though were streaming with tears, the thoughts in my head were full of *"what if she will never be able to anything"*, *"what if this is all she can ever do"* ………

But life went on of course. Amidst the anxiety, away from tick charts and goals, unhelpful, unasked for comments, ordinary day to day living was flowing. We had fun, laughter, play. Jake and Molly were both gorgeously natured children, I loved our time together as a family. In the moments I allowed myself to let go, to hang firmly onto the threads of my *wild wise self,* all the stress dropped away. We were, just a family. There were wonderous, fantastically awesome moments as life went on.

When Molly was three years old, one afternoon Jake, Lorna (a friend and neighbour) Molly and I were all upstairs. Jake and Lorna were playing Monopoly I think, Molly was sat on the floor and I was pottering.

Suddenly Molly stood up and started to walk, she was off.

Her delight was such that she walked at speed from Jake's bedroom, to her bedroom and back again, over and over, determined, strong, joyful. Jake, Lorna and I were laughing and clapping, tears of pure joy and love streaming down my face. She didn't want to stop, so we went downstairs and out into the street to take her first walk around the block to our friend's house.

We had waited what felt like such a long time for each of Molly's mile stones. And they happened in a very nonlinear way. She didn't bottom shuffle, she didn't crawl, she didn't cruise, she simply got up and walked when she was ready! She didn't make eye contact or hug us for a very long time. Now she hugs us all the time, she asks for hugs and gives them generously. I had read a post on FB which said, when we hug for 20 seconds or more there is a beneficial cellular change in our body. I don't believe everything I read on FB, but this sounded lovely true or not! I offered Molly a 20 second hug and counted out the seconds. The first thing she does now in the morning is to give me a 20 second hug, followed by many more throughout the day, bliss! And, her eye contact is deeply soulful.

A Movement That Threw Me A Life Line

We were fortunate that we lived in the catchment area for a pre-school, The Sophie Centre, which was inclusive! It had been set up by a parent of a disabled child, named Sophie, because her experiences of going to ordinary pre-schools was negative and she did not want to opt for special provision.

So, she created an inclusive play group – play and social interaction for disabled and non-disabled children *together*.

It started out in her front room, then as numbers grew, moved into a church hall and eventually landed in a purpose- built portacabin in the grounds of Dunraven secondary school – where Jake went.

The Sophie Centre was well established and respected by the time Molly was eligible to attend.

She started there when she was 2 years old. I had to attend with her (she was not yet walking and in nappies) until she was three and then she was supported by a one to one worker.

It was at The Sophie Centre I picked up a leaflet by Parents for Inclusion. This was a life changing moment. The language and feel of the information were in total contrast to all the messages I had been given so far from the specialist services. The overall message was one of *celebration*! I felt a tremendous sense of relief, of tribe, of hope, of belonging and of support. I contacted them that same day and before I knew it, I was at their offices in Vauxhall attending my first Parent Inclusion Support Group.

Parents for Inclusion had already been around for a number of years before I found them (specialist services had not signposted me to them). It too had been set up by parents of disabled children for parents of disabled children. Their aim was to be an ally to parents, to support them to navigate the educational system and know their child had a right to be included. They worked closely with The Alliance for Inclusive Education, headed by Michelin Mason, and with individuals such as Richard Reiser, Laura Chapman and Inclusive Solutions. They all worked within the Social Model of Disability.

It was this model in which I became an Inclusion Warrior. Through training, mentoring and friendship I rapidly became an Inclusion Group Support Worker for Pi, the Co-ordinator for The Sophie Centre and within a few years a team member of the newly established Early Years Development and Childcare Partnership for Lambeth.

It was 1999, local and central government were pouring money into early years provision and Inclusion was the buzz word. Two years later in 2001, The Special Educational Needs (SEN) and Disability Act was being introduced – practitioners, teachers and parents needed to be informed of and understand the new legislation. Educators also needed to be supported to understand how their practice could become inclusive.

I loved working for the EYDCP. It was brand new, the manager, Lisa, was fantastic. She said to me from day one that she knew nothing about Disability Rights, the new legislation or inclusive practice and therefore gave me a free hand to create a team of Inclusion Workers modelling the Social Model of Disability.

We were encouraged and supported to be

innovative and creative. I brought in Inclusive Solutions (still providing training and support to schools around the country) to train the team, as well as disabled people such as Laura Chapman and Michelin Mason, leaders in the Disability Rights movement. Jo Cameron, one of the founder members of Parents for Inclusion was my line manager. She was also a dear friend and ally.

I have deep gratitude for the wisdom and support she lovingly gave to me throughout all my years of knowing her. An invaluable piece of advice she gave me was to *"never do anything on your own Angie"*. This served me well on many occasions.

The Lambeth Inclusion Team delivered support to early years settings and schools providing inclusive tools and strategies for teachers to develop inclusive practice in the classrooms and for Headteachers and SENCO's (Special Educational Needs Co-ordinator) to develop Inclusion Policies.

We were received with mixed responses. The Social Model of Disability was a new idea for many, the message was loud and clear and extremely challenging to those people who regarded a disabled person as the problem (medical model) rather than their own attitudes. We came across barriers within the local authority too. I was not a trained teacher; my skills and wisdom were from the perspective of being a parent of a disabled child.

When I became the Manager of the Lambeth Inclusion Team, I was required to attend numerous meetings with members of the local authority and schools – from senior managers to educational psychologists to Statementing Officers to head teachers and SENCO's, some of who struggled with being required to think outside of the medical model.

I too struggled with their attitudes and the barriers they presented to parents and their children. For each parent I supported, the discrimination they were facing, was also my own. I had to learn to protect myself from daily rejection of ideas, comments and actions, all of which was a direct assault on the rights of my child to belong, to be included.

We did too work with teachers and local authority people who welcomed, embraced and implemented the social model. Many were relieved that at long last there was legislation, financial and practical resources to help them change policy and practice.

Under the EYDCP, the Inclusion Team had

several years of freedom to really make a difference to the lives of disabled children and their parents.

There were a number of excellent inclusive early years providers within local authority provision and within the private sector. A number of those had been inclusive long before it was a requirement by law! Molly had attended one such local authority provision, a Nursery that was only a 5-minute walk from our home and she was offered a place there when she left The Sophie Centre aged 3 years.

Her experience at the Nursery was largely really positive. Parents for Inclusion had been running an Inclusion Support Group there for a number of years and so there was a relatively easy relationship between nursery staff and parents. For me there was only one difficult moment that stands out in the couple of years she had there.

I noticed a new display of the children's work had been put up but I could not see Molly's piece displayed. I scanned the room and noticed her piece had been displayed completely separately and almost hidden from view. I confronted the class teacher who immediately became embarrassed and defensive. She made some excuse but I persisted in wanting to know why my child's work had not been valued enough to display with all the other children's work? And she had no reasonable explanation. I left in floods of tears.

The following day I was invited into the heads office to meet with the teacher and discuss the situation. There was an apology but the core of the statement that the teacher read out was that she was a highly experienced and skilled teacher, which she was, but that did not mean that mistakes can't be made and there is always more to learn!

However, I am pleased to say that after that incident the displays included all children's work, whatever their stage of development within their peer group.

It was important to make the challenge in these types of situations. Even when my adrenalin was urging flight, I had learnt to put on my armour and take up the challenge to fight for my daughters right to be valued and included.

There were numerous similar situations, and far worse, happening every day in some the nurseries and schools across the borough. I and my team attended countless meetings with parents, class teachers and SENCO's over those years.

One such meeting I was supporting a parent in, was for a review of a little boy who was about 6 years old and had a diagnosis of Autism. The class teacher was struggling to support him and was extremely defensive. She had a number of pieces of his work, which she used to attack his ability, because it did not match the ability of the other children. At one point she grabbed a drawing he had done and threw it across the table at the parent saying *"this is his standard of work; it's supposed to be a representation of an animal".* The parent's eyes filled with tears; she was speechless. I took the picture and showed the parent, saying *"Oh this is wonderful! Look at the colours he's chosen and how many marks on the paper he's made".*

What he had drawn was indeed beautiful and worthy of praise and celebration.

Modelling good practice was key to supporting both parents and practitioners. Offering inclusive solutions through, often very simple, tools and strategies (some of which I share along the way) supported the development of inclusive practice. With such support, communication between the practitioners and parents improved. Most importantly inclusive practice enables practitioners to support each child individually and the real bonus is that when the curriculum is successfully differentiated for one child, *all* the children benefit because teachers skill sets further develop.

There have been numerous practical tools and strategies I have used over the years in various situations to enable and empower Molly to be included and support those people who were providing her education. Here is one.

When Molly started at The Sophie Centre, I was given a 'Passport' to complete. The Passport was titled 'Hello, My Name is'. There were several sheets of A4 paper, each page had just a heading, the blank space was for me to fill out with various pieces of information about Molly. The information asked for was from a Social Model of Disability perspective. It was also welcoming and valuing the fact that I knew Molly better than anyone. For the front page, I was invited to put a photo of Molly in the centre. This instantly creates a person-centred approach, there she is, a human being, a beautiful little girl.

The headings on the pages were: - (I have put examples from Molly's Passport)

My Gifts

I bring laughter, playfulness and joy to the world. I

am unafraid to express my feelings. I am a teacher to all who are open to what I have to offer. My differences challenge people to 'think outside the box'. I help to communicate in ways other than speech and language.

Things I like

Music, singing, rhymes, hanging out with friends, my own space, festivals, going out in the car, having alone time in my car, going to gigs, Maggie's Barn.

Things I don't like

I sometimes get upset when people leave, especially when we've been having a good time.

Having my hair brushed.

Being asked to do something I don't want to do.

How I communicate

I have a lot of words, as you spend time with me, you'll get to know them.

I have phrases I like to use, for example "Shop's amorrow?" – this means "What am I doing today?" or "I want to see someone/go somewhere"

"Fall over!" – I love slapstick comedy and pretending to trip up makes me laugh

"Psst, psst" – this is from a story, I like you to hide behind my back and say "psst, psst"

"Come here!" – I want you to come with me, sit with me.

I will also let you know what I want by taking your hand and leading you to where I want to go.

<u>My Friends and Family</u>

Angie (my mum)/Rob (dad)/Jake (my brother) Tracy/Lee/Grace/Carmen/Jenny/Jane/Nev/MaraS para/Willow/Star/Claire/Bear/Scotty/Hayley/baby/ Ralphie

<u>How you can help me</u>

Eating and Drinking *– I can feed myself, I use a spoon and fork, not a knife. I can drink from a regular cup or glass. I do need you to chop my food up, just as you do yours. Hand me a tissue when I am finished and remind me to wipe my face. You may need to complete that for me but please ask my permission first before wiping my face.*

Sometimes I say "hungry" but I'm actually thirsty. Just check with me to make sure I'm asking for what I really want.

Washing *– I love having a bubble bath. I am*

happy for you to remind me to wash my body, handing me my flannel helps. Once you know I've cleaned my body I like to be left alone to enjoy my bath time in private.

Dressing *– I do need help putting on and taking off my clothes but I also like to try to do it myself (sometimes!). It does take a while to do these things, so mum makes it fun. She has made up a great song for getting dressed to. We sing it together every morning.*

Pull up your pants, do a little dance, get dressed today, hey, hey, hey!

Put on your top, do a little bop, get dressed today, hey, hey, hey!

Pull on your shoes, do a boogaloo, get dressed today, hey, hey,hey

Mum also asks me what I'd like to wear and shows me some choices.

Throughout the day *- I like to make my own choices, please ask me what I want to do or what I need. Be specific and use the words I know.*

Give me space if I am frustrated or angry, I just need a moment or two to express what I'm feeling and then I'm OK.

You may need to repeat something you say if I don't respond straight away.

Let me take your arm to link if we go out together.

Let me walk on the inside on a pavement, I don't have great road sense.

When we go to a café, once I've finished eating and drinking, I want to leave straight away – be prepared!

Communication *- **I love music** and need your help to put on my gadgets and change the songs. Music is really important to me, please take the time to make sure my iPod and speaker are charged and ready to use.*

I communicate with greater ease with music. I remember lyrics to songs and will often sing words and sentences rather than speak them. People who get to know me will sing questions or have a conversation with me using song, have a go, it's really fun and helps me to be involved and participate.

I always enjoyed filling out the pages, it was not only a celebration of Molly, it was also an invaluable inclusive tool for those people responsible for her wellbeing and education throughout her school years. Whenever she had a

75

new person supporting her, they would be given a copy of the passport as their initial introduction to Molly. The passport was not used as a substitute to us meeting to discuss support strategies, it was just one practical tool to add into the mix.

At the Sophie Centre all parents were given the passport to complete for their child and all parents were encouraged to involve their child.

When I filled out Molly's, I would offer her pencils and if she wanted to mark the pages she was encouraged to do so. I used her passport in many situations over many years, adding new pieces of information as she grew older and developed different skills. I still have her original passport somewhere up in the attic. It was lovingly saved; unlike all the reports, Statements, and Annual Reviews which were burnt in a ritual I did with friends before we left London to move to Wales. Very cleansing and healing!

What I loved about 'Hello, my name is', is that it gave me an opportunity to celebrate all that Molly was at each stage of her moving on from one setting to another. It was also fantastic too use when we started using Personal Assistants. And, although we haven't used it for a long time, I am now reminded as I write this that it would work just as well now as a document to go with my Will.

Creating your own Passport can be a very enlightening process and is also supportive to do prior to creating one for your child or an adult you are intending to help.

Even just thinking about the gifts you or another brings into the world is a fantastic starting point – have a go, honour the amazing person your child is. The amazing person you are.

Angie Northwood

The School Years

When Molly was due to leave Nursery School, Rob and I panicked. The thought of her going to a large mainstream school filled us with deep anxiety. Although I was already working for the Inclusion movement, and believed Inclusion was my child's right, I was scared – such is the power of the oppression. We knew we did not want her to go to any of the special schools in Lambeth, none were suitable, my experience of going to the segregated Mother and Baby swimming sessions at one of those schools cemented my view that somewhere else needed to be found.

I had heard of a small special school, very much like a mainstream school I was assured, (but of course it cannot be both!) and it was in Wandsworth. I started the process to request Lambeth funding through her Statement of Special Educational Needs for that school. I wrote strongly worded letters to support the request, saying we believed it was the school which would best meet Molly's learning needs and that as far as we were concerned there were no schools in Lambeth that could.

When I went to look at the school in Wandsworth, I was blindsided by the fact that it did *look* like a mainstream school. I was introduced to the Nursery Class teacher, she observed Molly for a few minutes and then said, *"We've never had one like that before".*

I was also told that Molly would be the only girl in the class with 6 boys, which the Headteacher expressed concern about. I chose to ignore the Nursery teachers comment and the concern of the Headteacher, still fooling myself I was making the right choice for Molly.

I find it bizarre now looking back at this decision, it was so far removed from what we truly wanted for Molly, it was in fact the opposite of what we believed in. But such was our fear that we somehow convinced ourselves it was the right choice.

Molly was offered a place and started in September 1998 aged 4 years. It didn't take long to realise we had made a wrong choice. Molly started chewing the sleeve of her tops, a behaviour she had not previously had, and was less vibrant than her usual self. Because Molly got bused to and from school, I never met any of the other parents, this was isolating and gave no opportunity to develop relationships for Molly.

I began to have serious doubts about the ability and attitude of the Nursery teacher and her Nursery Assistant. I was, for example, told by them that Molly was not allowed to use the alphabet cards because when she held them, she scrunched them up and when I was early to pick her up one afternoon (before she started being bused in) and found her alone in the classroom, I was told that she wasn't joining the PE class because she was afraid of the big balls being used. I was astonished by this and asked to see the Headteacher. She was appalled that Molly was being excluded from these activities and assured me she would talk to the Nursery teacher.

The final straw for me was witnessing the Nursery Assistant yanking Molly out the Assembly Hall and telling her off for spoiling the Assembly by not sitting still. She had not expected me to be there and quickly changed the tone of her voice, loosening her grip on my child's arm as I made eye contact with her.

I was paralyzed by what I saw and heard, unable

to move or speak. Inside I was raging and wanted to tell her to *"Get the fuck off my daughter"* and take Molly in my arms and run. But I was in fright mode, like a rabbit caught in the headlights.

Once home and weeping as I told Rob what I had seen, we made the decision to remove Molly from the school.

I then had the task to persuade Lambeth that the school we had been adamant to get her into was not right for her and that a Lambeth school could in fact meet her learning needs.

My friend and co-worker, Jo Cameron, asked me if I'd like to go and look at our local mainstream school and only a short walk from where we lived. My neighbours' children, Molly's friends, attended there, and it had a good reputation for being Inclusive. The Special Educational Needs Co-ordinator (SENCO) there had worked in partnership for many years with Parents for Inclusion, it had an Inclusion Support Group and Jo's son, who has Down Syndrome, had spent his primary school years there being well supported.

Remember that piece of advice Jo gave me *"Never do anything on your own"?* This was a perfect time to follow that advise. Caroline, another Pi colleague offered to come with me to meet the SENCO.

I was nervous, emotionally drained, desperate to find a school welcoming to Molly where she would be well supported and included. The SENCO was wonderful, she warmly welcomed me and listened to my concerns with empathy. I said at one point *"If you decide to offer Molly a place….",* she cut me off and said *"**Of course** we'll offer Molly a place, why wouldn't we! She can start straight away".* I burst into tears, the feeling to have the person who I perceived held all the cards, who was in the position of authority and power was unconditionally welcoming my child to the school, was of such great relief.

There was then the process of transferring the paper work and amending Molly's Statement of Special Educational Needs. She started before the Statement was in place I think, but the school accommodated her anyway.

We all decided that it would be appropriate and beneficial for Molly to start over again in Nursery class, recognising that to go straight into Reception would be too big a transition. This was perfect! Her friend Billie, who lived a couple of doors down from us was already in the Nursery class. It felt so wonderful to walk to school each morning with our neighbours, to our local mainstream school, we at last felt completely part of the community.

Sadly, the SENCO was moving on and the school was being modernised and merged with another primary school in the area. Her life at school started well but it was also a time in our lives when Rob and I were falling apart.

Rob had become depressed. On Molly's first day at her new school, we both took her there. Rob was so distressed and consumed with fear, he was fighting back tears and had to walk away. It was the first time he had been able to express the depth of what he was feeling but he did not know what to do with the emotion.

One morning just as he was leaving to go to work, he told me *"I'm moving out, I don't love you any more, I'll be staying at Rob Redlings"*.

I was furious.

I called him a coward. *"How dare you?"* I shouted. He said we had been miserable for years and he couldn't take it anymore. I started to pull photo's out of their albums of us laughing, on holiday, partying, playing with our children and I shoved them toward him. *"Look at them"* I cried.

He had made up his mind and he left for work.

I disintegrated into tears, my body was shaking, and, in my mind, I was working out how I would manage being a single parent.

Rob did come back that night and I showed him all the photo's again. This time though I had folded them to exclude him from the picture. *"If you don't love us anymore then go. I'll do this on my own"*.

He didn't leave. I asked him why he wouldn't see a counsellor, surely, he felt it was worth a try! He reluctantly agreed and made an appointment to see someone. I thought some time away to relax and let go would help him, I suggested he went to Glastonbury Festival with one of our friends. So, Rob went with an old friend of ours and his partner came and stayed with me for that weekend. Rob sent me a postcard while he was there. He told me he *did* still love me and that he wanted to be with me and that he felt happy and everything was OK.

I was really pissed off.

I couldn't believe he thought one weekend away had suddenly fixed everything and that the hurt I was experiencing was just as suddenly going to be fixed.

The counselling he did was pretty much the same,

a couple of sessions and he felt he was done. It was like a tiny plaster over a gaping wound.

But we did carry on and we *were* also very happy. We loved each other deeply. We didn't know at the time that what we both needed to do was look inside to understand that neither of us was to blame for the pain we felt. It was the oppression from having to fight for the right of our child to be included that was depleting us (amongst other wounding).

The school Molly attended was being modernised, all the children had to transfer to another local school, about another ten minutes' walk from home. Molly took all of this in her stride, she seemed to be enjoying going to school each morning, she had stopped chewing her sleeves and things were OK.

There were many obstacles though throughout her time in primary school. The merged schools did not have an Inclusive SENCO or Head, their staff had not experienced the inclusion of children who needed the curriculum differentiated in the way Molly did.

Picking her up one afternoon, one of the class room assistants supporting Molly came right on out with a classic statement *"I think she would be better off in a special school, have you thought about that?".*

By this point I had started to develop my external armour of Inclusion Warrior *"We've tried that thank you. We are very happy with her being in mainstream provision"* I answered cheerily. What I wanted to say was *"That's really not your fucking business and I didn't ask for your opinion – FUCK OFF".*

She was not alone in her view and frustratingly the new SENCO was a Medical Model authoritarian. I disliked her from the word go. I was at that time a parent Governor and was asked to be on the interview panel for enlisting the new SENCO, along with a community Governor and the new Headteacher for the two merged schools. During her interview, the soon to be new SENCO referred to disabled children as 'Handicapped'. An alarm bell rang in my ears. I did not warm to her at all, she had a 'no nonsense' approach to education. I heard nothing from her to suggest she had a holistic, inclusive approach or attitude.

I said what I felt as we discussed who would be given the post. I raised my concerns and felt instinctively she would be difficult for parents to work with. The Headteacher thought she would be a strong SENCO, the other Governor felt we would be able to offer her inclusion training within the school which could turn her attitudes and approach around. We had interviewed everyone else on the short list. There were no other applicants and the post had to be filled.

Against my intuition I voted with the Head and Governor to appoint her. Big mistake!

She was, as I had suspected, difficult to work with. She was SENCO for all but one year while Molly was there. At every Annual Review, a horrible review parents of Statemented children must endure, she attempted to persuade us at best, bully us at worst, to transfer Molly back to a Special School. It was exhausting to challenge her medical model views and practice, exhausting to have creative ideas to support Molly's learning disregarded so flippantly.

Molly had a passion for shoes when she was young. At home I would talk with her about the colour of her shoes, the style, we'd make up little dances and songs and rhymes about the shoes. She enjoyed these games, she was engaged, it was fun for us both and she was learning! When I suggested this practice be used at school, the SENCO told me it was not appropriate to encourage Molly's *'obsession'* with shoes.

Now, there's a word to trigger my rage. Why is it that if a child with learning difficulties has a particular interest in something it is labelled as an obsession, but when a child with no learning difficulties has a particular interest it is encouraged and supported and often a focus of pride for the parents and child.

Over the years I became adept at deflecting her negativity, I was well trained and versed in arguing my corner. I was experienced through my work, to offer Inclusive solutions to each and every 'issue' she raised. I knew experts in the field of Inclusive Practice who trained staff teams and local authorities and I pushed for their input at the school.

It was not only the SENCO who I had to do battle with. Some class teachers were deeply challenged having Molly in their class. The degree of curriculum differentiation needed to support Molly was outside of their experience. One class teacher, struggling to deliver what Molly needed, told me during an end of term review, *"I think Molly's lonely"*. The implication of this was that she did not belong in the class, "*surely, she'd be better off with children like her at a Special school"* she suggested.

I was in equal measure, both devasted and

angered by her comment.

Molly was not lonely. She had friends in her class and out of school. What the class teacher perceived as loneliness was in fact Molly's need to sometimes have time out, away from the frenetic energy of the classroom.

It was my role in situations like this to offer inclusive solutions. I would take a deep breath, bury the anger and tears and frustration, and offer what I knew. Time and time again, I was doing this not only for my daughter but also supporting other parents in my professional capacity at Annual reviews, Statement reviews, class reviews, training, Conferences, Inclusion Support Groups and in general conversations. It was exhausting, I was becoming depleted. I was sinking into depression.

I really needed my mother to be there for me. Her health was too poor for her to travel up to London, so when I could, I would go to visit my parents with Molly. On one such visit I had a terrible row with my mum.

Dad, mum, Molly and I were all sat at the dining room table having tea. I was telling them about a television programme I had watched focused on an innovative teacher helping young people who found school extremely challenging. I was attempting to make a point that when the curriculum is differentiated, teaching and learning opens up for each individual, but at the heart of what I was wanting to express was that I was finding the battles *I* was having to fight, exhausting and depressing.

My mum's response was to liken the skills of the teacher to going to a special school, which she knew was totally against my beliefs and that Molly had had a horrible experience attending one. I was furious with her. I screamed *"You never listen to me"*. I didn't want her to play devil's advocate, which she claimed she was doing. I needed her to say *"I hear you are hurting"* I needed her to wrap me in her arms, to agree with me, to see, to know, really know, that I was being treated like shit, that my daughter, her grand-daughter was being treated like shit and that it's just not right to sperate children.

But as I shouted, she retreated, all she could do was become a child herself, her inner child, her hurt child; her wounding was so deep she could not be my mother in that moment, she could not step up, she could not put aside her pain or even recognise that the pain I felt in that moment was also the pain *she* felt and that we were *both* deep

91

in our wounding. She simply wasn't able to be there for me in the way I wanted.

It was a painful process reading reports written by the professionals involved in Molly's education. From the moment she was diagnosed we had input from Home Support, Physiotherapists, Occupational Therapists, Speech and Language Therapists, Educational Psychologists, Special Educational Needs Co-ordinators and Statementing Officers.

Each of these people would write a report on Molly as evidence of what additional support she required in school, which in turn would place the additional funding into the school budget.

The focus was always on what she could *not* do as their primary concern. It is the same with the Benefit forms I still have to complete, although now not as frequently. These include, Employment and Support Allowance, Personal Independence Payment and the report required for Direct Payments.

With so much focus and attention being given to the 'can't do', many parents, including myself, become disheartened at best, depressed at worst. These negative views of our children are steeped in the Medical Model, regarding our children as the problem, rather than attitudinal and physical barriers.

I eventually acknowledged that I was depressed in 2007, when Molly was 13.

I was cycling to work along Brixton Rd one morning when I was knocked off my bike. I wasn't hurt, the man who knocked me down was mortified and drove me and bike home. I was in a daze and felt myself completely shut down. I am not surprised I was knocked off my bike, I was invisible, I had closed myself, my energy off.

Rob convinced me to go and see my GP. She was very kind and a good listener, the questionnaire I completed confirmed I was officially depressed. She offered me various options, anti-depressants, St John's Wort and counselling. I opted for St John's Wort and counselling, the later having an eight-month waiting list. I really couldn't wait 8 months to see a counsellor, so I searched the internet for a local private therapist who offered concessions.

About a week later I had my first session. I thought at the time I would be talking about Molly but as it turned out it was all about my mother. Until I healed my mother wounds, I would not be able to even begin to look at what I now know to be the 'After I'm dead' piece.

There were some significant light bulb moments for me in therapy. To begin with I realised why I was finding my relationship with Molly so difficult at that particular time. She was 13. My relationship with my mother disintegrated when I was 13. My mother's mother died when my mum was 13. For the first time I was able to see that my mums 'Map' ran out at that point because she had not been shown the way herself. She had been winging it, depressed, unsupported and numbed by drugs. I also *began* to understand why I was so triggered by loss of perceived control. This was tied in to feelings of abandonment, created when my mother was hospitalised, was shut down by the anti-depressants and her ongoing illnesses which prevented her from doing the things my inner child longed for her to do – to be fully present and hear me.

Home/School Diary

Because Molly had no speech and language when she was very little and a limited vocabulary as she got older, she was unable to tell us about her day at Nursery and then at School. There was often no time at the end of a day for her one to one support worker to have a chat with me. It was important for me to know what she had done during her day. How could I talk to her about it with no clue as to what occurred?

I wanted to help her develop her speech and language in a meaningful way, so knowing what she got up to each day, who her friends were, what she enjoyed, what she found difficult were all parts of a puzzle I needed to put together. A very simple, effective solution – like all-inclusive solutions, was to have a Home/School Diary.

Each evening I would write a few lines about what Molly had done at home. Her support worker would then be able to have a conversation with

Molly about it and tell her friends so they could interact with Molly in a meaningful way too. The support worker would at the end of her day, write a few lines about Molly's school day.

I was very clear from the outset that the Diary was not to be used to communicate any difficulties or moaning about any problems. Those issues would be talked about face to face at an appropriate time and space.

The Diary worked well, I began to know who her friends were, beyond those who were our neighbours. I could mirror activities she had enjoyed during her day and using simple sentences about her experiences I was able to slowly but surely build on her speech and language skills.

From using the Diary, I began to develop social story's for Molly and the school. The stories opened up a whole new world for Molly. She loved hearing back what she had done, she began to repeat words and then sentences and over the years she also learnt to recall stories from many years ago.

They are also used to help Molly understand specific situations she has struggled with. She has always found transitioning from one situation to another challenging. In the early days she would become very distressed and express her anxiety by shouting and sitting down, where ever she was! This happened for a long time at the end of a school day. I thought it was because she didn't want to leave school, but in retrospect I believe it was her way of communicating how tough the day had been, having to be still, to focus on things that made no sense and to be surrounded by so much energy and movement and noise.

I have learnt to recognise what is going on for her emotionally, I have used the stories to help her make sense of her experiences.

And they are also just for fun! Molly delights in hearing about some of her most enjoyable, fun or exciting days out and adventures with her friends over many, many years. I started writing her story books in earnest when we began to home educate Molly. I have lost count of how many there are, all very tattered from so much use. She also has a recording of some of her favourite tales, which she likes to fall asleep to sometimes.

The story books also provide new people in her life with a really great opportunity to get to know her, her likes, her dislikes, what she finds tricky, how we support her in moments of anxiety or frustration, her sense of humour, the places she

97

enjoys hanging out and who her friends over the years have been.

Suemagoo has been a family friend since Molly was about 4 years old. She and Molly have a close friendship and a mutual enjoyment of slapstick comedy.

Suemagoo Came to Stay

Molly's very good friend Sue was coming to stay for a long weekend. Sue lives in London, so it isn't very often that Sue, Molly, Angie and Rob get to see each other. They were all very much looking forward to the weekend.

On Friday afternoon Rob drove into Carmarthen with Angie and Molly to pick Sue up from the train station. The train arrived on time and there was Sue pulling her suitcase along the platform, looking out for Angie. They soon saw each other, had a hug and went straight to the car where Molly was waiting patiently for her friend. It didn't take long before Molly was laughing at all the funny things Sue started to say and do. She dropped her handbag onto her toe and exclaimed "Oh no, I've dropped it on my toe!" reminding Molly of the game they had made up together many years ago.

Once they arrived home, Sue put her things in the

Cwtch Caravan and then joined everyone in the kitchen for a cup of tea and a natter. All of a sudden a dastardly fly buzzed around Sue's head and she quickly swiped it away saying "Ugh no! There ain't no flies on me!". As she said this she slapped her arms and head and shoulders, pretending to swipe more flies away. Well, Molly thought this was totally hysterical and burst out laughing. Sue did it again, "Ugh no! There ain't no flies on me!", and slapped her self again and again. This joke amused Molly all weekend, she would join in with swiping the flies away and ask "Again, again"!

The following day they all decided to go to the beach, can you guess what Molly and Sue did on the walk down the hill? Yup, that's right, they played the "Ugh no! there ain't no flies on me" all the way to the beach.

That evening after a tasty risotto for dinner, Molly and Sue wanted to have a dance. So, some tunes were chosen, the volume was cranked up and the two friends busted some funky moves.

The following day it was raining, but that didn't stop Molly and Sue and Angie going for a walk. On went the wellies and rain coats and off they set with Barley the dog for a wet, wet walk. No one minded though because they were together and having a wonderful time.

That evening they had a quiet night of storytelling and songs and just a few more jokes before all heading off for a restful night's sleep as Sue was leaving early the next day.

In the morning, Rob, Angie and Molly drove Sue back to Carmarthen train station. Molly enjoyed rummaging through Sue's handbag one last time before they had to say "bye-bye, see you next time". And with hugs and kisses Sue was heading back to London and Molly, Rob and Angie were heading home to Cwmins.

Like all the inclusive tools and strategies I am sharing throughout this book, they are not only useful for a disabled child! They work for all of us – and that is the beauty of inclusion.

*Perhaps you could gift you and your child a beautiful notebook and set of pens. Invite them to tell you about their day and write it down as a story, or write down the key sentences or words, the pieces they are most excited about expressing, use **their** words as well as your own. Molly loves telling me her story in her own words and hearing me read it back to her. Creating and reading your child's story together can be fun, a time of closeness, quietness and connection.*

Home Education

I often apologise to my son Jake that we didn't home educate him. Some years after Jake finished university and was teaching, in conversation about education, he told me how much he had hated school. I honestly had no idea of the depth of his feelings. I knew that in both primary and secondary schooling there were teachers he didn't like and I knew he found the pettiness of the rules and regulations difficult. He was too, very aware of the many injustices that occur in school, which he found challenging. But I thought he was generally OK. He was a pupil who arrived on time to school, did his homework, got the grades the school wanted. But. There were occasions I challenged his secondary school for the way he was spoken to and treated. He was punished for dying his hair pink, told to take out his lip piercing (girls were allowed to wear earrings). He was told his appearance was a negative reflection of the school, *"You'll never work in a bank looking like that"*, stated his year tutor. He was made to sit in a room on his own all day because of the colour of his hair, whilst it was OK for teachers and other pupils who chose to bleach their hair or dye it any shades of 'ordinary' colours.

It is ironic that I spent so many years fighting for Molly to be included in school, when in fact both my children would have much rather been home educated.

Molly spent a lot of her time outside of the classroom, walking around the school building with her one to one Teaching Assistant. She needs to move, it's how she stays grounded, how she feels herself in her body. For a long time, she had almost perpetual motion.

With those teachers who did not differentiate the curriculum sufficiently, sitting behind a desk, having to focus on a subject that held no interest or meaning for her, being in class was a pointless exercise. So, she found her own way of coping being in the school environment, she left the classroom and walked.

She did too have teachers who were fantastic and differentiated the curriculum enough to engage Molly, they enjoyed having her in their class and always found her to be a positive influence on other children who were struggling in one way or another. And she did enjoy being with her friends in school.

I think the highlight of school for her, was the school leaving year trip away for a week. Her year group went to an adventure camp. Although the (difficult) SENCO was determined to find a health and safety risk in order to exclude her, Molly went. And by the time the trip came around a new, inclusive, wonderful SENCO had been employed. Molly had a brilliant time. She was very used to sleep overs and camping so she wasn't fazed at all. She had a go at everything and was especially thrilled with the abseiling. Here whole class stood at the bottom of the climb and cheered Molly on as she descended to rapturous applause as she achieved the whole descent. That week away, where there was considerably more freedom of choice and movement and learning through play, suited Molly.

When she was in year 5, the medical model SENCO was trying to have her moved to a Special School. Her reasons were that Molly had stayed a year down when she started school, and so, in year 6 she would already be secondary school age. In effect, if she stayed at her primary school, she would be doing an additional year.

The SENCO disapproved of this idea.

If she stayed though, she would move on to secondary education with her friends of 6 years. This made total sense to me, an additional year would be educationally and socially beneficial to her and she would move on with the familiarity of people she knew well from her class. The SENCO called a meeting to discuss *'the way forward'* for Molly's education. I put my view forward that staying an additional year would be the most beneficial route for Molly as well as being compassionate, kind and logical. The SENCO was pushing and pushing for a different outcome, *'special school is the way forward'* was almost dripping from her mouth. At one point I took a deep breath in to stop my rage and tears and stated "*If anyone suggests what I think you are about to say, I'm really going to lose it*"!

"But she'll start her periods soon" was the headteacher's bizarre reply.

Molly stayed the additional year. Her class teacher for that year was wonderful, he said at the beginning of the year he was apprehensive as he had not had experience in differentiating the curriculum in the way he was required to do for Molly. He loved having her in his class, he was also easy to communicate with, we worked well in partnership. At the end of year school leavers disco the headteacher came to speak with me. She said *"I owe you an apology Angie. You were absolutely right that Molly should stay. I am so glad she did. My staff have learnt a great deal about teaching having her in the school, she has been a real asset to us all."*

At secondary transfer age Rob and I were determined Molly would go to our local mainstream secondary school along with her friends from primary school. Several weeks before a meeting at the secondary school, we met with the SENCO from Molly's primary school, the wonderful inclusive SENCO and had been a joy to work with, to plan our meeting at the secondary school.

I had had to fight just to get the meeting at the secondary school, even resorting to introducing myself to the secondary school SENCO at a Conference so that I wasn't just another faceless name.

We went to the meeting armed with examples of Molly's work to demonstrate how she had been successfully supported and the progress she had made. The primary school SENCO came with us as an ally to speak on Molly's behalf as a professional. The three of us spent about an hour describing how well Molly had done, what an asset to the school she had been in relation to how teachers had improved their teaching skills, what a positive influence Molly was in the classroom and on and on…… After the hour of us speaking and the secondary school SENCO nodding and occasionally smiling we fell silent and she spoke. *"Can Molly line up?"*.

I left that meeting feeling 'dirty'. I had been trying to 'sell' my daughter to a woman who wasn't able to see or think outside a very tiny, securely closed box.

Rob and I decided to rethink what would be next for Molly. Did we really want another 6 years of battles and stress? Did we really think the school system would provide Molly with what would enable and empower her? If the issue of lining up was the only thing the SENCO was bothered to ask, was she really going to support Molly to be included. Would the school model good practice to help the other students to be inclusive? The reality was the school did not want Molly.

We concluded we did not want the school, any school, for Molly.

With that thought put out into the universe I 'happened' to meet a woman whom I had supported in the past. I asked her how things were and she told me she was now home educating her son. I had not heard of home educating and was interested. She advised me to look at the Education Otherwise website, where I would find all the legal information I needed, templates of letters to local authorities and head teachers and lots of testimonials from parents about the home education experience. I felt so excited I almost ran home. That evening I started researching what I needed to do. The website was brilliant and the stories from parents were incredibly moving. I sat with tears flowing as I began to vision a new path for Molly and for our family. Rob was equally enthusiastic and we began the process of deregistering Molly from school.

She would stay at her primary school until the end of the school year and instead of transferring to a secondary school, which was unlikely to happen anyway, unless we opted for a special school and we were definitely NOT going down that route again, we would embark on home education. Fortunately, because Molly was in mainstream provision it was a relatively easy process to deregister her from school.

If she had been in Special Education, we, her

parents, did not have the right to deregister her without the local authority's permission.

The secondary school did actually offer Molly a place, even though I had told the local authority Statementing Officer we were going to Home Educate her. The offer was for her to attend 1 hour per week. That's not a typo, that was their offer!

In Lambeth, parents who home educate are monitored by the local authority. Because Molly had learning difficulties this included an Educational Phycologist as well as the home education officer. There is no financial support, not even when your child has a Statement of Special Educational Needs, so no help with resources of any sort. Parents who Home Educate their children save their local authority a great deal of money.

Because I had worked in the education system for a long time, I knew what the local authority officers would be looking for at their monitoring visits. I knew what language to use and how to present what Rob and I were doing to support Molly's development and how to present Molly's progress. For us, it was then, a breeze. It was actually a joyful experience, the local authority officer and Ed' Psych' were extremely supportive of what we were doing and impressed with how Molly was clearly benefitting from our approach and practices.

She flourished away from the narrow confines of school. We all did. It was such a huge shift of energy. Not having constant battles, endless meetings and reports, negative attitudes and approach allowed us to begin to relax, to let go of other people's projections, we had space and time to enjoy and have fun with learning and teaching. It was wonderfully liberating.

My experience of home educating was indeed a freeing of institutionalised thinking and practice. It was about listening deeply to my child, noticing what she enjoyed, what interested her, what she disliked or frustrated her. It was about knowing what her energy levels were, especially when she started menstruating (I will go into more detail about this later on), allowing her to sleep or just 'be' when she needed to.

Rob and I decided we would share the home education and in order to do so we both worked part time. It was not an easy adjustment and not without its own forms of stress. It took us all a while to shake off the structures of school times and lessons. Molly would put her hand up in the air if we asked her if she wanted to do something!

It was scary going to the home ed' groups not knowing anyone and not knowing if people would welcome us or if Molly would be included by the other children. So, as liberating as it was on many levels, for a period of time I felt extremely isolated and lonely. The network of support I had created and had access to throughout all of Molly's school years didn't exist in home education.

Eventually though I found my tribe and made good friends with one particular woman who had a daughter about the same age as Molly and they got on well. Cherilyn was an amazingly vibrant and loving woman. She introduced me to the magic of the moon and the power of the Divine Feminine! She was also an ally to me and Molly at the Home Ed' groups we went to, she would challenge any discriminating behaviour whoever it was directed at and by whom!

It was also Cherilyn who told us about a Home Education Camp held in west wales each year at a site called Pencraig Farm. We decided to go along and have a break from routine, we were seasoned festival goers and campers and excited to be experiencing home education further afield.

We were welcomed by Helen and Amanda, a couple at that time, who owned and ran the small community. They were wonderfully and naturally inclusive and very consciously asked if there was anything more they could do for us or for others in the future, as their intent was to be Inclusive to all.

We were unaware at the time that a seed had been planted during this visit, a seed that has now blossomed and flourishes.

We continued to home educate until we moved to wales and at that point Molly was turning 18, there was no longer a requirement to continue to do so. Of course, she never stops learning. We still use rhymes and song and dance, her interests, (no longer shoes, it really wasn't an obsession, it was a passing passion) such as music and story's.

We continue to learn with her, noting what needs to change, what needs to be done differently, whose company she thrives in, whose company she finds challenging, what activities she no longer enjoys, finding new activities that interest her.

Rob and I can still only work part time, we constantly have to juggle our days, playing tag team for the various and numerous things we need or want to do. Mostly we manage our basket of responsibilities well, we both enjoy our work, we love where we live, we have become much better at having time to relax and have fun, as a family, with friends and just the two of us.

And yet, there are still strong echoes from the school years, which I only realised this morning while folding some laundry. As I folded the clothes, in my mind I was thinking about what I needed to tell Jenna (Jenna is a PA and was hanging out with Molly over the weekend) before Rob and I went out for the day. *"Shall I leave the clothes out on Molly's drawers in case she needs a change, rather than put them in the drawers, because then they'll be easier to find"* I pondered. Then the thought *"She'll find them if I put them in the drawers, she'll find them if I leave them here"* dropped in.

And I had a sudden realisation. All the notes and instructions I give or leave for friends, or PA's or even Jake, that I continue to do, are an echo from those school years. The echo being my worry. Worried that everything had to be as *easy* as possible for the teachers, the support staff and yes, even friends and family for fear that if it wasn't easy, they would reject Molly. Molly's access to school was always on the condition that it wasn't too difficult for the school.

So, I didn't put the clothes in or on the drawers, I left them where they were.

I let it be.

I let the relationship between Molly and Jenna be.

I let go of a behaviour which no longer serves me. The worry did not actually exist, it was just an echo.

PATH - Planning Alternative Tomorrows with Hope

Soon after we started Home Educating Molly, I called in Inclusive Solutions to facilitate a PATH for her. Colin Newton and Derek Wilson are ex Educational Psychologists who for many years now have supported the inclusion of children and young people into the education system and also adults into their communities. I learnt how to deliver PATH's, trained by Colin and Derek, when I was Inclusion Manager for Lambeth EYDCP. I knew having a PATH for Molly would be immensely supportive to our whole family as we began our new adventure of home education.

The purpose of a PATH, is to provide a 'plan' for a positive future. The process involves looking at what exists at that moment, what the individual would like in their life - this is the dream part, no limits, it invites creativity, thinking outside the box, innovation! Then, what and who needs to be called upon to manifest those dreams. And lastly, those people who are there for the PATH process are invited to 'sign up' to committing to one thing to support the PATH process in action.

I invited our family, our friends and Molly's friends. Our front room was packed, it was a hot sunny day, I felt excited and very emotional as I introduced Colin and Derek to everyone. Colin facilitated the gathering, inviting each person to contribute ideas, what they knew about Molly, how they saw her in the future. For example, Jake said how beautiful and photogenic his sister is and thought she could be a model. A friend Scott spoke about how he saw Molly enjoyed expressing herself through movement and how much she could teach others.

While each person spoke, Derek drew images on a huge piece of paper stuck up on the wall. By the end of the process we had a visual representation of the process.

Various commitments were made too during the PATH process, as well as outside of it. We were blessed to have all sorts of offers of support, offering different things. I'm listing some of what Molly was gifted as examples of what you can ask for – but remember it's all about what your child likes and wants.

Anne, Molly's Aunt, is an amazing artist and has a beautiful, gentle soul. She offered us support on many occasions over the years. She stayed with Molly and Jake several times so that Rob and I could go away for a weekend. She also invited Molly to Yorkshire, where she lives, to spend a day making art. Rob and I had a gorgeous day walking in the hills with my brother Mike, while Molly and Anne had a wonderful day having fun with music, material and dancing.

My mum committed to writing to Molly once a month to share her news, knowing Molly loved storytelling and because she was unable to come and visit us due to her health issues.

Bev, an ex-drama school friend, came to one of the Home Ed' Groups Molly and I went too. I was feeling isolated there and her friendship made all the difference to going.

Debbie, another of my ex drama school friends, invited Molly to walk her dog Toby with her. This became quite regular and Molly really enjoyed the responsibility of walking Toby and loved the cuddles!

Sue who has known Molly since she was 4 years old, and is a dear friend to us all, has a very special relationship with Molly. She has always gifted to Molly her playfulness, her love and laughter.

In later years Rob and I used the same PATH process, with just the two of us, to dream into our plans for moving.

Why not have a go at creating a PATH for yourself, a friend or your partner?

Is there someone you know who may benefit from having a PATH?

Be courageous and share this wonderful inclusive tool with anyone you are aware of as being excluded or isolated.

If you feel a PATH would be right for you or another and you need the professional, experienced input, contact Inclusive Solutions.

The Importance of Community

When Molly was very young and I was just learning to navigate my way around the oppressiveness of the system, I found it difficult to imagine Molly having a social life. Thankfully, we chose well in where we moved to from Battersea. Wingford Rd in Brixton was a beautiful community. We moved there when Molly was 10 months old and Jake was seven. We quickly got to know the family at No 13, Ortrud, John and their 2 daughters Moira and Lorna. The children grew up together, Jake and Lorna were the same age and were close, Molly too had a close relationship with Lorna in particular. We shared Christmas's together, each year choosing a theme for fancy dress and each of us cooking a Christmas dinner and taking it over to one or the others house to share. We always ended up partying into the night, filled with laughter and a great deal of fun. Paul, Sitali and their daughter Davita from No 15 were also part of this annual celebration and also very dear and close friends.

When we started home educating Molly, Sitali and Davita would often hang out with us, I have very happy memories of our time spent together with our two gorgeous daughters.

We were also good friends with The Millers, who lived at No 25. Julie and Tim had three children, Sophie, Billie and Jacob. It was through Tim and Julie that I met a very dear friend, Bernie and her daughter Molly. It was at one of Tim and Julie's kid's birthday parties, Molly and Molly were both on the swings and Bernie and I started chatting, we instantly clicked. Bernie was a Social Worker and at that time was working in Adults with Learning Difficulties in Lambeth. After Molly and I had left the party and returned home there was a ring at the door, it was Bernie. She said to me *"I'd like to put my money where my mouth is and invite Molly to come over to my house to hang out with my Molly once a week".* I probably burst into tears, I can't remember strangely, but I do remember feeling so happy and a shift of energy taking place as that relationship developed.

Bernie was true to her word and she is still a special friend to this day even though we now live so many miles apart and rarely see each other. Molly did indeed go over to her house once a week for **years** and as Bernie and I became closer we spent many Saturday evening's or

118

Sunday lunchtimes and a few holidays all together.

There were also lots of party's in our house. In fact, Rob and I hosted some cracking good gatherings over the years in Brixton. Molly loved these social events and, in those days, she stayed up with us all into the early hours!

She also enjoyed a weekly hang out at Tim and Julie's. Every Friday afternoon after school she and Katie and Emily (neighbours from around the corner) would descend on the Millers! These were very happy times for us all. At about 6pm I would go and join Tim and Julie, as did Sarah, the mother of Katie and Emily, bottle of wine in hand, for an evening of political discussion, great food, music and lots of laughter. This too continued for years.

But as the children became teenagers' different interests and experiences were unfolding and Molly was getting left behind. The same was happening at Bernie's. Her daughter was feeling pressured to be friends with Molly, when she really wanted to be doing other things. Fortunately, there were a couple of girls from Molly's school class who had independently chosen to be Molly's friend. They often came to our house to hang out and have sleep overs and

119

we'd also take them all off for trips to the coast and country side in our little VW (we'd bought another one by then!) on the weekends. One of those girls, Ashleigh, now of course a young woman, has stayed friends with Molly. They have known each other since 1999, when they were 5 years old.

I am deeply grateful for the friendship, support and love we received from our Brixton community. They were all very important to my wellbeing, my sanity at times, and truly significant in how Molly perceived herself in the world. She was welcomed, included and loved without question, organically and authentically.

It was painful when Molly's friendships dropped away. She wasn't able to pick up the phone or text a message to arrange a night out. She wasn't forming new friendships or having girlfriends or boyfriends. Her friend Ashley had moved away too. It felt as if everything I felt safe in, because Molly had a life, was crumbling. It was time for change. This was a key piece to us making the decision to leave London and move to Wales.

The 5 Keys to Inclusion

When I trained with Inclusive Solutions, I was taught an inclusion tool they created called the 5 Keys to Inclusion. Each heading is used to invite parents or practitioners to consider what they may need to change, create or expand on in order for individuals or groups of people to be included.

I went on to use the 5 keys on many occasions in different scenario's, including training early years practitioners, parents and volunteers and staff in social settings. My training partner, Sue Utley, and I made lots of bunches of large laminated keys, with one heading on each key. Post training the keys worked really well, as parents and practitioners were able to have this invaluable tool in their bag or hanging in the classroom or at home to refer to when doing their planning.

Looking at the five headings, why not have a go at thinking about what you or someone you know may want or need in each heading if e.g.

- *You were moving to a new location*
- *You were starting a new job*
- *Your child was starting at an after-school club*

Welcome: What things make you feel welcomed? What would be problematic to encounter when arriving?

Listening: How do you feel if you are not being listened to? Are there specific things which help you to express what you need to say? What key issues do you want others to hear from you?

Long View: How often would you like to check in with what you are doing? Do you see yourself in the same home/job/club for a long time? If you do, what is important to you in order to have longevity in where you are or what you do? For a child, what will happen next when e.g. the age of your child means they have to move onto a different club for their age group?

Gifts: Do you know what your gifts are? Are you able to let others know what your gifts are? How would you like to use your gifts?

Team Work: Who do you like to help you when you need assistance with something? Do you find it difficult asking for help? What could another or others do to help you?

Learning: How do you learn? Are you an auditory learner? A visual learner? Do you need to move around in order to take in information? Do you like to reflect or dream into information?

Take a look at Inclusive Solutions website for more details on the amazing 'range of inspiring inclusion orientated services' they offer at **https://inclusive-solutions.com**

A Life with PA's

Something wonderful happened a year into home education. When Molly was 13 years old, we applied for Direct Payments. DP's were introduced by central Government because disabled people fought hard to have policy change. The Medical Model provided disabled people with archaic provision and resources – e.g. Day Centre's where a person has little or no choice in what they do there or home 'care' suited to the carer not the disabled person – arriving at the same time every day and leaving at the same time every day, giving no freedom of choice to the person it is supposed to assist.

Direct Payments have gone a long way to readdress these types of situations. Designed by Disabled people for Disabled people, DP's are all about providing what an individual wants and how they want it delivered. How DP's worked for Molly changed our lives.

Molly wanted to be out and about, going to café's,

going to festivals, hanging out listening to music, shopping – all the usual things a 13-year-old young woman wants to do.

She did those things with us and family friends, but the reality was she didn't want to do those things with us, not *all* the time anyway. And it was exhausting for us, physically and emotionally. Molly couldn't just pick up the phone and ask a friend to come over or arrange to go out – I had to do that for her. And most of her friends were in the school system, they weren't around during the week days and as I said before those old friendships were falling away.

Because we were home educating at this point, we all really needed support from other individuals. Personal Assistants, funded through Direct Payments sounded like a great solution. The process involves having an assessment from a Social Worker. Molly had no need for one up to that point, so it felt strange and somewhat intrusive having to be interviewed by one.

The assessment took place in our home, Rob and I were asked various questions in relation to what Molly liked to do, what sort of assistance she required and what her difficulties were. We also had an opportunity to express how exhausted we were and that we needed this as much as Molly.

Once we knew the application for DP's had been

approved, we went ahead and advertised for a Personal Assistant. This was liberating. The nature of DP's was that Molly and we would choose who the PA would be and what she would be employed to do, the job description was written by me and totally reflected what Molly wanted and needed, it was from a Social Model perspective – of course!

We were fortunate that Roehampton University was not too far from us and it had an abundance of young women who were looking for part time work. I looked into how we could place a job advert on the campus website, an easy process and the wheel was set in motion.

Molly's first PA was someone Jake knew, he was in his second year at Roehampton, studying Human Rights and Journalism and recommended his friend to us. Her name was Charlena and she was a gift from the Goddess! We held an informal interview at home, Charlena had written a great application, very Social Model, and so we were excited and optimistic she would be suitable. But the most important issue would be, does Molly like her? Molly gets on with most people and she is also a very astute judge of whether someone has a compatible energy and attitude. Charlena most certainly did. She and Molly got on brilliantly. They both had a love of music, a great sense of humour, and Charlena had no barriers to learning how to communicate with Molly. She was confident, outgoing and had a natural ability to sense when Molly needed space or quiet time.

For the first few weeks Rob and I would go out with Charlena and Molly while she learnt the practical things she needed to now in various situations. She learnt that going to cafes was a favourite social activity for Molly. It was important to know that queuing to pay is difficult for Molly, so it is best to ask to pay at the beginning. It is also advisable to get your own drink in a take away cup because when Molly has finished her drink, that's it, she wants to be off. It's sensible to have Molly sit on the inside of the table so that when she is ready to leave, she can't just get up and run off, which she would do, she has to wait for you to gather up coats and bags, help Molly on with her coat if it's cold or raining and then you can head off together. These are really simple logistical things that avoid any sort of anxiety for Molly or the PA. In short, simple adaptations that make everyone's lives run smoothly – an excellent Social Model example.

One PA was not enough though. Molly had 25 hours per week, this is too much for just one person to do and too intense for Molly. So, the post was advertised again at Roehampton and another two wonderful young women were employed. Molly 'H' and Natalie completed Molly's first 'team' of PA's. They were each very different in personality and brought very different gifts and skills. Molly developed unique relationships with them all.

While we were in London Molly had one other PA who joined the 'team', Sasha who was a local Brixton woman, and had a young daughter who also got to know and enjoy Molly's company. The relationships were not just restricted to them being PA's. Charlena and Molly H introduced Molly to their friends and she was invited to hang out with them on numerous occasions. Charlena and Molly H also became very close family friends and we enjoyed many social gatherings with them. Charlena came to a number of festivals with us and spent the first two weeks here at Spirals when we moved to Wales, to help Molly settle in. Molly H had moved to Australia while we were still in London, but we keep in touch via Facebook and when she was last in the UK, she came to visit us here, as has Sasha and her daughter.

Arriving in west wales, as wonderful as it most certainly was, meant we had to apply for Direct Payments all over again. It was very frustrating and, in my view, totally ridiculous that her 'care plan' could not just be transferred. Molly was also due to move into the Adult Services section that May as she was turning 18.

Molly missed her London PA's and the independence and freedom it had given her. I too found this transition really difficult. My old trigger of abandonment kicked in big time as I was also dealing with my own loss of my friendship group and support network.

Fortunately, Ceredigion Social Services acted very swiftly. We waited for a very short amount of time before a Social Worker was allocated and an interview assessment date booked.

The assessment and interview were actually very painless, the Social Worker was a lovely young man, who had also only recently moved into the area, he was supportive and enthusiastic not only about Direct Payment's for Molly but what we were aiming to create here at Spirals. The assessment was approved and within a relatively short time frame Molly had her Direct Payment in place.

Recruiting PA's here has worked very differently to our experience in London. The reality of living rurally is, that there are far fewer people here, no university close enough to be viable to recruit from and who ever we do employ has to have a car. However, it has been the case that we have found all the PA's very organically.

We found Molly's first PA here through a person we had purchased some slate tiles from. He then came for massage treatments with Rob and as they chatted, he said he knew a young woman who he thought would love the role of being a PA to Molly.

So, I got in touch with her and organised an informal interview here a few weeks later. Fran and Molly got on brilliantly. Fran was energetic, enthusiastic, confident and fun. She didn't have a car but at that stage of the game we decided it was worth having to pick her up and drop her off home each day.

It was still the case that one PA was not sufficient, so we continued to advertise for a couple more. Molly's second PA here was working in a local seasonal café. I popped in to ask if I could put up a notice and a young woman behind the counter took the notice, read it and *said "I'd like to do this!"*. A third person was found, again in a local café, in exactly the same way. Just as it had been in London, each woman brought a different energy, gifts and skills.

Over the last seven years here, Molly has employed some great PA's. A few have stayed for long periods of time and all developed wonderful relationships with her. A couple have become close family friends and one is about to reconnect with Molly now she is no longer working and has free time to hang out with her as a friend.

About a year ago though, all the PA's dropped out of the scene for various different reasons and to me it felt like death. I was heartbroken and totally at a loss as to what to do next. But it was, of course, just the life, death, life cycle and we were in the phase of transitioning into something new.

Molly had got sick to death of going out to cafes, or trips to town, or for walks and even with hanging out with her PA's. Her PA's noticed this and it was becoming increasingly tricky for them to manage, as Molly was being very clear that she did not want to spend time with them.

I on the other hand was burying my head in the sand and ignoring both Molly's and the PA's wisdoms that something had to change. As each PA resigned and we were left with no one, I simply had to pull my head up out of the sand and look inward for my own wisdom.

When having a PA works well, it works really well! Molly has had so much fun with all her PA's, and they with her for many years. The following story is a beautiful example of how PA's can support Molly's social life experiences.

Dub Pistoleroes by Laya

It was a dark January evening and Molly was all dressed up, ready for a night out. At 6pm she heard the broom broom of Laya's little white van arriving. With a shiver and a quiver of excitement she grabbed her bag and set off with a whoosh into the night.

At Pencraig Farm, the two women found Finn in the static, and a delicious smell of chicken cooking in the oven. Molly relaxed with some tunes playing until it was time for dinner. Suddenly there was a knock knock on the door. Hello? Who could it be? At the door was Molly's friend Emma. She was so excited to see Emma that her cheeks flushed pink and she let out a loud, glorious laugh. Emma sat down, but Molly needed to let her excitement bubble out, so she walked to the bathroom, giggling and shivering and quivering! She felt somehow this was not wild enough, and so feeling the pull of the full moon, Molly went outside and 'howled' with joy as she felt her feet go squish and squelch in the mud – ooops.

"Gosh Molly, would you like some dinner now?" asked Laya.

"Yup, yup, yup" answered Molly. So, the three women and Finn munched their delicious food, although Molly couldn't eat much as she was still

131

so excited.

A quick snuggle with Emma and then it was time to get into Felicia the van and set off to Narberth to see The Dub Pistols. When they arrived, the hall was already packed with people and thumping, pumping tasty bass of music filled their ears. The 3 women got in past the queues to the front and Molly tried to go straight out the back door. "Wrong way Moll's" Laya laughed as she showed Molly the way to the hall. When she turned back to Emma and Molly they had disappeared! "Oh no" thought Laya. She did a quick circuit of the hall looking out for Emma's top hat and Molly's style of dancing BUT, that evening everyone was wearing a top hat and dancing Molly styley. In the dark hall with all the steam punk fashion, Emma and Molly were unspotable. Laya asked the doorman if he had seen Molly, he hadn't but said he'd keep an eye open for her. Then Laya spotted some of Molly's friends but none of them had seen her either, so she headed back into the hall and suddenly spied her two friends by the sound desk having a standing cwtch. "Phew" thought Laya. The 3 women were very happy to see each other and had a steam punk dance to celebrate, the music vibrated through their bodies as they shivered and quivered to the boom of the bass.

A little later on they made friends with the security guard called Kim. He joined Laya in a game of stopping Molly making a beeline for backstage. "Nnnnnn, no Monkey Molly, not that way" they laughed.

When Molly felt tired, she and Emma had a rest on a handy chair, and when it all felt a little too crowded and stuffy, Kim let Molly and Laya out the backdoor to get some fresh air. Outside, the two friends were wrapped up warm in their coats and went for a stomp in front of the building. They stomped up and down the pavement laughing and whooping with excitement, then back inside they went for a stomp up and down the corridor, making the door staff laugh at their antics. They were having a wonderful time. It was getting late by now but no one was ready to go home yet, so Laya called Rob to let him know they wouldn't be home for a while longer. The women carried on with their games, the falling over game, the bump game, the yawning and laughing game and making friends with other people at the gig. Eventually they ran out of energy and decided to head home to Cwmins. They said "byeeee" to Emma and set off with a whoosh and "beep, beep "down the dark country lanes in Laya's little white van. At last they arrived to the welcome lights of Cwmins, Rob was still up waiting to greet them, it was past 1am, so Laya sad "night, night" and Molly went straight to bed, content, exhausted and ready for a restful night's sleep. What an awesome night out.

Little Things Which Make a Big Difference

Many years ago, we were on a family outing in Camden Town. We came across a retro boot stall and Molly was excited to go in and have a look. She saw all the different boots on the shelves and picked a few up, touched others and then decided to sit down to have a longer look at one particular pair. She was calm, content and clearly loving the experience.

The woman whose stall it was did not like Molly sitting on the floor, or that she had taken a pair of boots from the shelf. We sensed her disapproval and gently suggested to Molly that we move on to another stall. Molly had not finished her experience though and wanted to stay longer.

The stall owner became aggressive in her manner and told us to leave her stall. Molly then sensed the woman's disapproval and she felt anxious. We felt anxious. But we knew if we pushed Molly to stand up and leave, she would become even more anxious and the situation would become messy.

We tried to explain to the woman that Molly would soon be finished and we would go. She persisted though and created a really difficult situation. Molly was feeling embarrassed and angry that she was being told to leave and demonstrated her feelings by refusing to move. In my head I was telling the stall owner her behaviour was discriminating and unlawful. We had NEVER been asked to leave anywhere before this.

Rob and I managed eventually to persuade Molly that we had to leave and on we went. No one had offered us any help during the altercation. There were plenty of sideways looks, a few distinct looks of disapproval and even support for the stall owner.

We were shaken and deeply hurt. If just one person had offered an act of kindness and compassion it would have helped us to manage the situation with less anxiety, which in turn would have helped Molly to feel less anxious, which in turn would have enabled us to leave more quickly and more gently. We would have felt less judged and isolated.

Even better would have been the stall holder welcoming Molly's interest in her goods. Perhaps engaging in the experience, asking us what size boot Molly takes, what colour does she like, showing her boots she might like.

I learnt a great deal from that experience. At the time I was not equipped enough to challenge the stall holder or, even better, to engage her and model to her how the situation could be handled differently! If the same situation occurred these days I would know instantly how to engage or disengage.

Not everyone is open to learning. Not everyone is in a place of opening or awakening. And in kindness to the stall holder, who knows what was going on in her life in that moment of time.

I have learnt there are some battles worth 'fighting' and others are definitely not worthy of my energy or time. And in those scenarios, I have learnt how best to support Molly so that she is not distressed.

All parents or friends of parents will recognise those feelings of being judged when their child is having difficulty in managing a situation. The public can just about manage to ignore a *child* in melt-down but when it is a young person or adult with learning difficulties in melt-down or simply being who they are, some people stare, make uninvited negative comments or show their disapproval. And this is really because

a. the situation is likely to have triggered their own stuff in relation to being 'a good girl/boy' and

b. because when the general public see someone behaving in ways that are not familiar with, they retreat, it's outside of their experience, they don't know what to do.

Which is proof of the point I make, that segregation perpetuates lack of understanding, perpetuates fear, perpetuates the belief that 'that person' doesn't belong.

And all of this brings me back to how important, how crucial community is, how belonging, participation and inclusion are the ingredients for changing lives for the better. Everyone's lives become better, not just the person who is vulnerable to isolation and discrimination. Because when we open ourselves to kindness and compassion, we open ourselves to love. I have been told time and time again how Molly has empowered and enabled individuals to effect transformation in their life. How they have learnt 'to be in the moment', to invite laughter and fun into their day, to be unafraid of fully expressing themselves.

If we had taken the road of segregation or to hide Molly away, those individuals would not have had the opportunity to receive the gifts Molly brings to the world. She would not have had the opportunity to belong in her community, to participate, to be included.

As I write this, I can feel my energy shifting, I can feel my solar plexus firing up. I feel so passionately about creating inclusive community. If we all give just a little of our time and energy to consciously participate in creating inclusive community, to ask a person if they need anything, or pop over for a cup of tea, or go for a walk, then fewer people would be isolated and marginalised. Everyone benefits when we consciously create community.

When I read this section to Rob, he reminded me that on the same day, still in Camden Town, we visited another stall that was selling Egyptian jewellery with some very beautiful delicate pieces. Molly went in, Rob and I were still feeling the upset of our previous experience and asked Molly not to touch anything. The woman smiled and said, *"Come in, it's fine, don't worry"*. She spoke to Molly directly asking her if she'd like to sit next to her, which Molly did. They sat together, effortless, a mutual enjoyment of each other's company. The stall holder was genuinely pleased Molly was interested in her goods, Rob and I were superfluous to their interaction, we simply were not needed! Such a different experience for us all and in Truth, for us it is far more typical than the negative boot lady encounter!

So, when we witness a person in distress, a simple act of kindness can make such a difference. A smile and asking *"Is there something I can do to help?"* Or, offering to carry their bags to the car, something, just something to express non-judgment, compassion and kindness.

Of-course this takes courage and it may be that the offering is rejected. But if the *intent* is only to be kind, then how the act is received is not important.

It has taken me a long while to reach a point where I do not instantly feel my child is under threat or being undermined. I was asked a question while writing this book on my FB group Soul to Soul, following a post I shared in relation to how autism is regarded in another culture, specifically the Maori culture.

"The Maori word for Autism is "Takiwatanga". It

means "In his/her own time and space".

I responded by writing, that even though Molly doesn't have Autism, I liked and related to that description. A friend was clearly surprised, thinking Molly is Autistic (which many people do). My friend asked *"What **does** Molly have?"*

It's not the first time I have been asked this question and probably not the last! In the early days, when Molly was very young, not so young, teenager, young adult, so I suppose up until recent years (let's say around the last 6 or 7) I would have felt triggered, angry, upset, or frustrated being asked this question. On that day though, I felt none of those things. I knew immediately how I would answer the question; I was even pleased I had been asked the question. So, this is how I answered

Angie Northwood: Ok, so I know what you're asking here. I am going to answer this with integrity and from a place of absolute Truth.

What does Molly have? She has fun, she has friends, she has a great sense of humour, she has times when she is sad or angry or frustrated, she has times when she is so full of laughter her sides could split, she has a love for life, she has wonderful insight into what her body needs when she's mooning, she has moments when she is still and centred, she has times of dreaming and visioning, she has a label called Global Developmental delay and Hypotonia.

That label actually tells you little to nothing about who Molly is though. Nor does it tell you what sort of support she may need or how you can best communicate with her. It is a label like any other label - leading to assumptions and stereotyping, putting her in a box with others who have the same label but are nothing like Molly or she like them.

What does Molly have? She has a gift of teaching others that we do not need labels to know each other. We all simply need to get to know each other.

Thank you for asking your question Jenna, by asking you gave me the opportunity to give a different view point and another paragraph for my book! Love it. Love you.

Jenna Chapman: I knew you would answer just like this! Hehe. Love it! Completely agree and understand! Thank you for such a great answer

Angie Northwood: Awesome, thank you for the prompt!

Molly develops her friendships a lot through humour, Jenna got to realise this quickly and observed how much she also enjoys rhymes, funny noises and sounds as they chatted.

'Snort' – a story by Jenna

Molly and Jenna walking through the woods

Molly looking through Jenna's bag, looking for goods!

With a snort she laughed (make a snort sound)

You're having a giraffe!

Know what Jenna, I think you're reeeeally daft.

Have you thought about how a small act of kindness may make a big difference to someone in your community?

What could that act of kindness be?

Do you have a friend/s who would be interested in joining you to talk about community inclusion?

Angie Northwood

So, How Did We End Up in West Wales?

In 2011 Rob and I were getting itchy feet, London was feeling too small, opportunities for Molly were dropping away. Fear of growing old and not being able to afford being in the City, we could both feel an energy that was sitting deep inside us, trying to be unblocked to allow it to flow.

We decided to buy a large Mercedes van, to convert into a camper and spend time offering our therapies at festivals and do some more travelling. We found what we wanted on eBay and Rob caught a train down to Bournemouth to have a look at and hopefully buy the van. He fell in love with it, had a quick test drive, paid the asking price and set off home. The van was fantastic, big enough to create a double and a single bed, a kitchen, have a wood burning stove and still space for Barley our dog. Rob spent all his spare time building the interior, people in our street were really interested and would stop and chat with him about what he was doing and our plans for freedom and adventure. Rob did such a great job and we were thrilled with the end result.

That Spring I applied for us to go to The Green Gathering festival in Chepstow to offer our massage therapies. Rob was already an experienced Sports Massage Therapist and Jake and I had both recently trained together and qualified as Holistic Massage Therapists. I promoted us as a family business. Sue and Sue who organised the Healing Field liked my application and were extremely supportive and welcoming. I called Sue to say we would also need tickets for Molly and her Personal Assistant. There was no problem with this and in the Summer of 2011, Rob, Jake, Molly, Charlena and I set off for the Green Gathering.

On the morning of getting ready to leave, packing up the van, full of excitement and joy I suddenly felt very unwell. All my energy drained from me; I could hardly move. There was no way I was not going, so I slept in the bed in the back of the van all the way there. On arrival I crawled out of the van, still feeling grim and told Sue I didn't think I would be able to work. She was amazing, saying *"Well what better place to be than the Healing*

Field, don't worry, rest". So, while Rob and Jake sorted out pitching our bell tent in which they would give the treatments, Charlena and Molly went to explore the site, I rested.

The following day, in front of the bell tent, I created a little space with cushions and rugs, and I set out my Goddess cards. I sat and watched and listened to all that was going on around me. Over the days we were there, many people stopped to chat with me, I had never given myself that amount of time and space just to be still. It was very beautiful to experience and it opened something up inside me. I could feel the blocked energy beginning to flow.

A therapist came and sat with me one morning. He told me he was planning to do a walking pilgrimage in west wales where he had bought a small piece of land to build a round house. His ancestry, like mine, was Welsh and he felt a strong calling to connect to his ancestors. As he spoke and I listened, I felt my energy shifting again, something powerful and important was dropping in. And, because I was still, I was listening deeply, I was feeling, my heart was open and was ready to receive my own wisdom. This was the moment everything was about to change for me. It was the beginning of my transition, the beginning of letting go, of diving deep, of my death and rebirth.

That evening my body was vibrating, I said to Rob *"What are we doing? We have to make our move now or we'll miss the boat!"* Rob was equally as excited and we could feel the beginnings of a new adventure, one that we had dreamed of and tried to do on several other occasions but this felt different.

We had another significant meeting at the festival. Helen and Amanda (from Pencraig home education camp) were there with the Magical Youth Theatre and we bumped into Helen one afternoon while strolling through the site. We were pleased to see each other and she was genuinely interested in what we were doing and how Molly was getting on. It was great to reconnect and be reminded of the welcoming, inclusive, loving people we had met in west wales. We returned to the Home Education Summer camp that same summer and met Rose and Kenny. They had recently moved to west wales and I was keen to ask what their experience was and if the community was inclusive. I only got to meet Rose on this occasion, she was so enthusiastic about their move, the community and really reassured me that we would be welcomed and there were lots of inclusive opportunities for Molly.

This was an important experience for me. Rose was so genuinely warm, welcoming and supportive, which she and Kenny continued to be while we were looking for properties and beyond.

Back in London we set the wheels in motion. Our house in Brixton was gorgeous, we had invested a lot of love and energy into it and had had very happy years there. We didn't however feel any sadness about putting it on the market, another sign that we were indeed ready to move on. We painted and finished off bits and pieces that even after 19 years we hadn't got around to doing!

I had loved living and working in Brixton, the nature of my work meant I was deeply immersed in the local community and knew many folks from many areas of Brixton. And, the road we lived on was a truly wonderful community. We had our dear friends who I would greatly miss and it wasn't until we got to Wales that I realised I would grieve for the loss of them being close by.

So, the house was looking fantastic and we put it on the market. It took only a few days for several offers to be made, everything was going smoothly. We spent hours looking on the internet for properties in west wales within a ten- mile radius of Pencraig Farm as our starting point. We were fortunate that Rose and Kenny had settled into a house in Pencader, within our search range. They were so supportive to us in our search and put us up in their spare room on one of our final visits. We had already made a couple of trips up the motorway to look at properties but none had been right.

We had made an extensive list of what we wanted, with the intent of being as self-sufficient as possible, creating a space for our healing work, community and opportunities for Molly and with the possibility of Jake coming one day and building his own home on the land. Each time we viewed a property we had a clearer idea of what we really wouldn't compromise on and what we were willing to let go. The more we looked the more I knew what was important to me – trees, water and being in a valley.

There was a specific moment that my connection to my ancestors and this land filled my Soul. We were looking at an off-grid house, really small, too small for our needs, facing North so no good for growing food and too far from a village or town. So why did we even look? Well, there was something which kept bringing me back to reading over the details and although we knew it wasn't going to be the one, we also knew there was something there we needed to see. It was grey, pouring with rain and rather cold the day we visited the house. The owners were lovely and welcoming and we chatted about each other's dreams and plans for the future. Rob and I then ventured out into the weather and were drawn down into one of the fields. At the bottom was a stream and a copse of trees. As I stood gazing at them, I felt my heart open and my whole-body fill with life force energy. Of course, I'd seen streams and trees before, but I received a really strong, clear message from them in that moment, I had to be near both, they are what makes my Soul sing.

On our last visit to view properties, last for a while anyway as we had exhausted all that there currently was to see, we stopped off in Llandysul to buy a few provisions for the long journey home. Molly was with us, sitting patiently in the back of the car. The only space to park on the little street was right outside an Estate Agent. I popped into the local Spar and Rob got out of the car to look in the estate agents window. I returned with cookies and crisps and water, tired and ready to head home. Rob passed me some details of a property which had literally just gone up in the window. It was over budget and I hated the look of the interior, *"Oh no, I don't like this, it looks horrid"* I said dismissively passing the details back to Rob. *"No, look at the land, the outbuildings, it's got everything we want!"* he said, passing the details back to me, urging me to look again.

We went into the Estate Agents and asked if we could go and see it immediately. Frustratingly, they had no one to show us around, so we arranged to come back on the following Friday, a whole week to wait but we had work commitments so we just had to be patient. A long, slow week passed and Rob and I set off at the crack of dawn, on our own this time, to view what became our new home in wales.

As soon as we started to drive down into the valley we fell in love with where we were. There was something magical, calming, mystical. It was raining again, grey and still cold, perfect weather to do a first viewing in – if you fall in love with something in that weather you know it's going to be incredible in sunshine! And Rob was right, the land was beautiful, there was a stream, a woodland, outbuildings and even a converted little cottage ideal for a holiday let, which is how we intended to make a living until we were established as therapists.

And it was perfect for Molly. More perfect than we could have imagined until actually living here.

The space here for Molly is ideal. She can open any of the doors to outside and wonder off. As long as the gate to the track off the land is closed, she is safe. She has a huge courtyard to walk in, 3 fields and the house has space for her to move with ease and pick and choose where she wants to be.

Having choice has changed things for Molly. She has little restriction here, a great deal more freedom here than she could ever have had in London.

So, we moved to wales, just seven months after having made the decision to leave London. We were in equal measure, no longer afraid of moving into the unknown and completely terrified of moving into the unknown! But we had had a light bulb moment, 'If things don't work out, we'll do something else'. This made a huge difference to how we approached the unknown, this attitude really empowered us to do it! We didn't know how we'd make it work other than believing we were making the right choice.

On March 23rd 2012 we arrived at midnight in our new home. The sky was clear and filled with stars, Molly got out of the van, looked up at the sky and said *"Ooooh ahhhh, lovely stars!"*. The weather was totally gorgeous for the next 3 weeks, hot sunshine, and a wonderful introduction to rural country living.

What sensations do you feel when you think about making a change in your life?

Where in your body do you feel them?

Have you considered what holds you back from stepping into the unknown?

What may help you to shift from any blocks or restrictions?

Womb Wisdom Wise Woman

When I left home at 18, my mum's health had already slowly but surely declined. She was a fighter, she was determined not to give in to her illnesses, but she fought the battles she would never win. She chose to put her faith in the doctors and specialists who only ever prescribed drug, after drug after drug. Each new drug or different dosage created new layers of illness, each one exacerbating the previous.

London was only an hour or so away from Colchester, so I was able to visit fairly often and when an emergency call came, of which there were many, I could get to my parent's home relatively quickly.

By the time we left for Wales many years later, mum was blind and couldn't get out of bed. Dad was her 'primary carer' and their relationship was strained. Mum considered herself a burden, dad was exhausted.

Between arriving in Wales in 2012 and my mum passing in 2013, I had made 2 emergency visits, each time thinking 'this is it'.

On April 15th 2013 my brother Anthony called me mid-afternoon to say mum was dying, he wasn't sure if I could get there in time to say goodbye. I ran outside to find Rob, tears streaming down my face, I intuitively knew this time it really was 'it'. Molly's PA Fran was here and was able to stay with Molly while Rob and I headed off to Colchester.

It was a long drive, we sat mostly in silence, I felt like a little girl with the words, *"I want my mummy"* going around and around in my mind.

On arriving, my brother Anthony was just about to leave, he couldn't bear being there any longer, he didn't want to witness her passing. Rob and I went upstairs to mum's bedroom. My older brother Mike and his wife Anne were already there, dad was in the room next door. He too was finding it unbearable and couldn't be in the same room as mum.

Anne had been lying next to mum, she got up to let me take her place. For the following 6 or so hours I lay next to mum, stroking her head, holding her hand, talking to her. She was heavily sedated with morphine; I don't know what she was or wasn't aware of. But it didn't matter, I knew on some level she *was* aware of us all there and that it was a comfort.

In the very early hours of April 16th my mum passed. We had called dad in when we realised she was taking her final breaths, he stood awkwardly by the bed and held her hand. When she stopped breathing, dad looked at the palliative nurse and asked *"Is that it?"*. He left the room; we all left the room.

I stayed with dad for just over week, it was the longest time I had ever been away from Molly and Rob. We were both in deep grief and muddled our way through each day. Between Anthony, Mike, Anne and me we managed to sort out the myriad of tasks that have to be dealt with after a death.

At mum's funeral, I thought I was going pass out, I wanted to howl and scream and beat my chest, I wanted to fall to the ground and weep until I disappeared. But I didn't. My son Jake put his arm around me and held me close as we walked into the crematorium. I managed to read the words I'd written and talk to people at the buffet afterwards, and then I went home, with Rob and Molly, to Spirals of Wellbeing, our new, beautiful, healing home.

Dad and I were the closest we had ever been during that week we spent together and continued to develop our relationship after I'd gone home to Wales. He told me a close friend of mum and his had had a psychic experience shortly after mums passing. Dad was bemused and baffled as to why mum was not communicating with him. He had never explored or practiced any sort of spiritual connection, but I was sensing his grief was opening him to the possibility. I offered to share with him a poem I had written after receiving a message from mum during a poetry dive in a Women's Circle. He was keen to read it and I was very moved that he showed an interest, it was something very special we shared together.

About a year after mums passing, dad had finally made a decision to have a knee operation. He had been in a lot of pain for a long time, walking was becoming increasingly difficult. He didn't have the operation while mum was still alive, fearful that if anything went wrong, he would not be able to care for her. I was visiting dad while he was making his decision, he showed me all the literature and asked me what I thought he should do. He was clearly worried, scared actually, so I listened and held him when he cried.

The knee operation was successful; however, he

suffered a stroke in the recovery room. His recovery from the stroke was long and slow. He spent about 3 months in a rehabilitation hospital, to begin with it took 3 nurses to help him just sit up. My younger brother was convinced he should go to a Nursing Home, he couldn't imagine dad ever being well enough to go home. Dad, on the other hand, was determined he *would* return home. His feelings were that going to a Nursing Home would "*finish him off*". I was 100% behind my dad, whatever he wanted I would support him in.

He did go home. He had several carers who came each day to help him with cooking and cleaning and his self-care. On one level he enjoyed the carers coming and going, he formed a close friendship with one of the women, and it was certainly less lonely than it had been since mum died. Dad spoke of driving again and hoped to be able to go on holiday at some point. The reality was though that he was now living with poor health and much reduced physical ability and he was extremely lost and lonely without mum. He was also becoming forgetful and often didn't take the correct dosages of his medication. He started to hide that he was frequently falling, fearful that this would lead him to living in a nursing home.

And then, what felt like very suddenly, he became extremely unwell and was admitted to hospital. My brother called me to say it was serious and dad was unlikely to recover. Me and my 2 brothers spent the following week watching dad die. It was awful. He was struggling to breath and his right arm was in perpetual motion. It looked to me like he was trying to release blocked energy. When I had alone time with him during that week, I sang him the 'seven tones of love', a chakra practice to bring balance and flow to the chakra centres. The first time I sang the tones to him he turned his head toward me and just for a nano second, I felt he connected with me and had a moment of stillness and peace.

I was distraught when dad eventually passed, not so much because he died, but because his death had been traumatic and the closeness we had allowed in, ended. I learnt a valuable lesson from my dad about the importance to heal. He never did do his inner work. He became angry, bitter and ill from his resistance to look at what he needed to heal and I believe this contributed to his difficult passing.

He had been dedicated to my mum; she was his one and only love, but because he refused to meet his shadows or ask for help (because he believed real men don't do that) he also resented her. When he became depleted from caring for her (over many years), he was on occasion nasty to her. This must have been so painful for them both. My mum told me about this, I asked her if dad was mistreating her, she assured me he was not but she also knew they needed support before the situation worsened.

During mum's final years I believed we became very close, which on one level we did, but the relationship was unbalanced and I gave out far more than I could really manage. When I moved to Wales, I spoke with her *every day*, *every* phone call was full of her pain, both physical and emotional.

In that first year of being in Wales, her final year of living, I was experiencing my own disintegration but never allowed myself to open up to mum and ask for her help. I was a *'dutiful daughter'*, a *'good girl'*, I kept my own problems to myself. I came to recognise that I chose to take on the role of her mother. I subconsciously thought that by giving her the love and nurturing she had not received from her mother (because she died very young), I would receive the love and nurturing back.

But she knew nothing of what was going on with me, because I didn't tell her. It was with the onset of my menopause years that I was eventually able to begin to heal my mother wounds.

Walking a Transformative Path
My Menopause Experience

I found my life cycle phase of Enchantress (peri menopause) was the call to step onto a Path of Transformation, into my authority, into my sovereignty, it was the time of peeling back the layers, diving deep into my shadow world, listening to the voices rising up within, the voice of my inner child, the voice of my mother self, the voice of my ancestors. For me those voices were soft whispers, roaring banshees, screaming heart and womb wounding, encouraging me, urging me, supporting me and holding me as I crawled and strode, scrambled and flew, cried and laughed, raged and gently soothed myself as I wound and wove my way toward Crone.

In the early stages of menopause whilst still in London, I became very aware of all my upspoken, unexpressed rage. I would feel intensely emotional and have a deep need to cry or scream, which I didn't do. I was intolerant of other people's behaviour or demands. Before I started 'doing my work' and looking at my shadows, recognising the behaviours which no longer served me, diving into the murky, muddy, uncomfortable Truths, before I started acknowledging any of this, I was needy; by that I mean I was *afraid to ask* for what I needed, afraid to expose my vulnerability, afraid I would lose control or be rejected.

I chose to put on a smile and say *"I'm fine"* in a high-pitched tone. A lot of the time I was fine, but often I was not.

So, at this point I was not taking ownership of *my* 'stuff', I got angry with Rob, angry with myself, because I didn't know what was happening. Because I was disconnected to my womb, to my female life cycle, to my menstrual cycle, I was not accessing my innate wisdom, my intuition. I was not honouring my *Wild Woman*. I am amazed at my resilience, strength and will power to get on with all the external stuff I was dealing with.

My body was giving me clear messages that I needed to pay attention to. It was my womb, unsurprisingly, that had the role to bring me back to myself, to bring me back to, as Clarissa Pinkola Estes calls *'The one that knows – Wild Woman'*.

Some months before we left London, right in the mix of selling, looking for somewhere in Wales, giving up work, packing and the rest, I had a very painful and very heavy period and I had also been needing to pee a lot. I was in so much pain I called NHS Direct, my 'go to' at that time. The nurse I spoke to gave me good practical advice, basically to make an appointment with my GP to check things out. I didn't. I was too afraid. Any indication of illness threw me into internal panic, sure I was going to be diagnosed with Cancer, that I would be told I was dying.

I chose to ignore the messages my body was giving me. I understand why I responded in this way. I grew up with a mother who was frequently ill, who disappeared into hospital and modelled to me 'not to make a fuss'.

So, I didn't make an appointment with my GP.

On my birthday, just a couple of months before we were due to move, I called NHS Direct again. I was experiencing the feeling I could not breathe deeply enough, that I wasn't getting enough oxygen in my body, I was extremely anxious. This time I was advised to go to A & E. Rob and I headed off to Kings Hosp', where we spent a fretful few hours waiting to be seen. I was taken to a bed in a ward and had my blood pressure tested

165

and my heart monitored. The doctor asked me if I was worried about anything, to which I replied *"no",* genuinely believing I wasn't. He told me all the tests were showing everything was as it should be, my heart was really very healthy. He didn't know why I was experiencing the breathlessness and feelings of panic. What he didn't ask me, was anything about my cycle or if I was peri menopausal, he had been told my age after all! Being totally unaware of peri menopausal symptoms myself, I made no connection to the painful, heavy bleed, nor to my bouts of anger, my anxiety, restlessness, insomnia and tiredness.

I was also unaware that women's kidneys have to work much harder than normal during menopause and this can cause breathlessness. I learnt from my acupuncturist in very recent years that this is to do with the Chi energy. (So now, as well as having regular acupuncture sessions, I also drink lots of nettle tea, to nourish my kidneys and support my immune system, particularly through the winter months). I was sent home from hospital, none the wiser but relieved I was given a bill of health!

As I began to land in my new home in wales, I had an awakening. I began to breath more deeply; I began to feel alive in a way I had not previously experienced. I also began to feel my disintegration, all that I thought I knew, who I was, what I was doing, it all began to fall away.

The trees, the stream, the air, the expansiveness of the land and her healing energy shifted my Soul vibration. But the dissonance of having moved from the vibrational state I had been in, to that which I was now moving toward, felt overwhelmingly uncomfortable.

The polarities of being felt confusing and exhausting. There were moments I was so full of joy I would raise my arms to the sky, feeling that life was so beautiful, so wonderful and in the *same* moment also felt utter despair for the state of the world.

I was so very happy to be in magical, mystical west wales. These were not just words - I could *feel* the magic and the mystery, I felt like I was home but didn't know what that really meant.

I was also grieving for the loss of my friendship circle in London, for the loss of the familiar and therefore comfortable.

I was angry that I would now have to go through the process of registering Molly with Social Services again in order to access Direct Payments. I would have to find new PA's in a

167

landscape I had no knowledge of. I would be navigating from scratch.

Molly too was missing her friends and her social life supported by her London PA's. When Charlena left, who had come with us when we moved in, Molly and I struggled with our losses. We both felt lonely and being responsible for creating her life opportunities filled me with resentment, anger and a deep longing for support.

Rob and I were struggling with each other and unaware I was peri menopausal. All the shadow pieces we had both ignored for so long were screaming to be acknowledged.

About a month or so after moving to Wales, I had a conversation with Rose. I was still concerned about needing to wee all the time and was aware that something was 'not right'. Rose told me that she knew someone at one of the Home Ed' groups who knew a woman who did healing work. I chose to do two things.

1. to go and get a diagnosis from my GP and
2. I spoke with the woman at the Home Ed' Group and she directed me to Jules Heavan's. I looked her up on the web and gave her a call to make an appointment.

My GP had referred me to the hospital for further

investigation. He tried reassuring me that it was probably nothing but better to have it checked anyway.

When I spoke to Jules, she was very clear that she would not heal me, that I would do that myself. She would offer me her wisdom and healing tools to empower me on the journey I was about to step into. Rob drove me down the M4 just beyond Swansea for my first session with her. All the way there I could feel my energy shifting as the years and years of unexpressed, unacknowledged rage, fear and pain bubbled and boiled. Torrents of tears were building in my eyes and a primal urge to howl lay trapped in my throat. As I entered Jules' yurt for the first time, I was also entering my own temple, I was taking my first awakened step into reclaiming myself as a powerful woman.

That first session with Jules was the beginning of a five-year transformational journey. It was also a period of time in which Rob and I grew further and further apart, whilst at the same time, we were working really hard to get our business up and running, settle into our new home, find PA's for Molly, get to know people, find our place in the community.

To begin with and for several years into my inner

work, Rob found what I was doing very threatening.

There was an occasion when Jules came to our home to hold a singing Circle up in our Chalet. It was a Women's Circle and about 6 or 7 women, plus myself were attending. After the Circle we all came down to the kitchen for a cup of tea. I introduced Rob to everyone, and all sat or stood in the kitchen chatting. I became very aware of Rob's energy. I glanced over to him and saw him looking at me with such suspicion. I felt very uncomfortable, for a moment or two thinking I was doing something wrong. And then I realised, he was seeing a 'me' he did not know. He was witnessing me in my transformation, with the women who were holding me.

And I get it now, how that must have felt for him. Women in Circle, in a process of change, are potent! There really is magic when we come together to heal, to explore, to discover and be in our authority.

Something very powerful dropped in for me. I was not afraid of my potency! It also reminded me that we, women, have been persecuted for our potency, punished for coming together, killed for standing in our authority. So that look of suspicion was also powerful and why for that moment or two

I thought *I* was doing wrong.

In early summer 2012 I had my referral appointment and went for a scan of my womb and to see the Consultant Gynaecologist. I apparently had a very large Uterine Fibroid. My first reaction to my Fibroid, was to banish it! I told Jules I had written a mantra to my Fibroid, it read,

 "I do not want you; you are not welcome; I do not need you".

Jules said *"Those are very strong words"* and then through her gentle questioning and guidance I began to realise that my Fibroid was not an enemy to be got rid of. My Fibroid was there as a wakeup call to reconnect to my womb.

And so, I started to develop a relationship with my womb. I sang to her, I cried to her, I walked and talked and danced with her. As I worked with this practice, I was again aware of an opening, a deeper awakening. I was beginning to feel not only my connection to my womb but also to my ancestral mothers and sisters. The heavy bleeding and pain ceased. The need to pee frequently decreased. So, by the time I saw the Consultant again I was able to say the symptoms that had led me to have a referral were no longer present.

171

At the first appointment with the Consultant and at all subsequent ones over a period of about 3 years (I was monitored every 3 and then every 6 months) *every* time I went I was offered a Hysterectomy, even though I told them *every* time I was in *no* pain, my bleeding was *no longer* heavy, I had no other symptoms other than wanting to pee more frequently during the pre-menstrual and menstrual phases of my cycle when my womb was naturally enlarged.

I was staggered, outraged actually, that I was offered an intrusive, major, life changing operation even though I was in no pain or discomfort and apart from the Fibroid, my womb, ovaries and cervix were completely healthy.

There *are* situations when a woman does need a hysterectomy, but when it is not a life-threatening or intolerable situation there are so many avenues of healing to be explored. I am so enraged that it is still the case though that our wombs are chopped out as a *first* option.

Because I was 52 and still had a regular cycle the Consultant also considered me to be older than 'normal' to still be bleeding. Actually, women enter their menopausal years at very different ages, if you are ever in any doubt, I recommend Susun S. Weeds book *'Menopausal Years. The Wise*

Woman Way'.

I continued to work with my womb wisdom through various different practices. Jules introduced me to Poetry Dives, The Naked Voice, sitting in Circle, rituals and celebrations. I dived deep into my Soul to explore my hidden Shadows. I was shown how to work with my Shadows, to understand my triggers and peel off the layers of behaviours which no longer served me.

While I worked with my changes guided and held by Jules' wisdom, I also developed my knowledge base and skills through training. I did an online course on Working with Dreams and Working with Chakra's. I studied Reiki levels one and two with a local gifted Reiki practitioner. I became a Moon Mother, specifically working with the Divine Feminine energy to practice in Womb Blessings and Womb Healings. Jules ran a course in which I became a Soulful Facilitator and most recently I discovered Soul Realignment and qualified to become a Soul Realignment Practitioner.

Each of these pieces of study were an integral part of my own healing and transformation. Each one unlocking another level of connection to myself, others and to Earth.

Unlocking and working with my womb wisdom

empowered me to relate to Molly's cycle with more awareness and compassion. It has been a truly beautiful experience for us both. Molly always intuitively responds to her body's needs during her cycle. She has taught me so much in relation to honouring my body and my cyclical nature. I was beginning to note on a *Moon Cycle chart where she and I were in our cycle and what each cycle brought for us. Because I was going through the menopause by this point, my cycle was erratic, but I was also now very consciously connecting to my life, the moon and season cycles.

Charting Molly's cycle has made life easier for us all. We work with the female archetypes of Maiden, Mother, Enchantress and Crone. These relate to the four phases of a woman's menstrual cycle as well as her life cycle. We weave those into the moon cycle and the cycle of the seasons.

Molly is in her Mother phase of life. I see this in her lovingness toward me and others. She chooses to express her nurturing, soft, gentle and loving nature by hugging me and kissing me gently on the head and snuggling next me to listen to a story or have a chit chat. Her eye contact has changed, she looks more deeply into my eyes and without words we speak the volumes of love we share as mother and daughter. It is truly beautiful. We were sitting at the kitchen table the other afternoon, Molly glanced over at me and we took a quiet moment to look into each other's Soul. And there we sat, just for a short time with the biggest grins on our faces in our mutual understanding and sharing of our wise and wild woman selves.

Molly's menstrual cycle is pretty regular. She has a Moon Chart on her wall to track her cycle and on which I can record how each phase is for her.

Her Maiden phase (pre ovulation) is pretty easy going. She has energy and a lightness of being. Her appetite returns and life flows along.

Her Mother phase (ovulation) can sometimes be a little tricky and I wonder if this is to do with her ovulating. It is the time when we often feel most potently sexual and I can see that this is still something Molly is learning to be with.

Her Enchantress phase (pre-menstrual) is really easy to recognise. She becomes ravenous, she doesn't stop eating! And she has no difficulty in expressing the build-up of tension. She often shouts at us, becomes frustrated and angry, she may burst into tears and she slams doors repeatedly! I honestly celebrate this; I am pleased that she is able to express what she is feeling and because we do not try and stop her expressing what needs to be released, the moment passes swiftly. She has learnt that she can take herself off to her room to be alone and be angry. When she is ready, she'll accept a hug and she moves on.

These observations have served her and us very well. We have learnt that in her Enchantress phase it is not sensible to plan trips out or have too much going on at home. Her energy levels are low at this time and she needs space and crucially the freedom to express herself in the safety of her own home, there is no pressure on her to behave like a *'good girl'* and no danger that anyone will judge her or label her behaviour as *'not very nice'* or *'aggressive'*.

In her Crone (menstrual phase), Molly is brilliant at honouring her body and spiritual needs. She slows right down (she is usually very active) and becomes dreamy and quiet and still. I can actually see the moment she drops into the Crone phase. She asks for a hot water bottle and often takes herself back to bed, just for a while, until she feels ready to be up and do what she chooses to do. Her appetite falls away too, this is so useful to know as I no longer worry that she doesn't want to eat. This phase lasts only a few days. She is very aware of the flow of her blood and asks to have her pads changed. She sleeps much more deeply and I have learnt it is helpful to wake her as I go to bed so that I can change her pad before it becomes too full and really importantly so that she can empty her bladder, because when she sleeps as deeply as she does in this phase, she doesn't wake herself up to go to the toilet.

Being womb wise with my daughter is significantly important to how she is supported to express herself throughout her cycle. If you have a daughter or are still menstruating yourself, I strongly urge you to have a go at using a moon chart and to read '*Wild Power*' by Alexandra Pope and Sjanie Hugo Wurlitzer.

If you're not still bleeding, noting how you feel throughout the moon cycle can be incredibly supportive in how you plan your days.

Practices for womb wisdom

A note about Rage! I was never, until very recently, able to express my anger or rage in any way other than tears. Through sitting in women's Circle's and specifically learning the practice of The Naked Voice, I did at long last find a way to express that particular emotion. The rage is never physically aimed at others. Using a method that allows and empowers me to access my rage has also shown me those things I wish to change within. As a consequence of that, I am also empowered to make the changes I wish to make externally. I am unafraid of my rage, knowing it connects me to a deep wisdom, and I regard it as a spiritual resource for healing. This has been invaluable throughout my peri menopause journey.

And, I also use 'softer' practices such as the following.

<u>*Singing to my Womb*</u>

When I started working with my womb wisdom, I created a daily practice of singing to my womb. I would take myself down to the fields and walk and talk with my womb, and a song came in.

I made up my own tune and the simple words fell in.

I've come to sing a song for you

I've come to sing a song for you

I've come to sing a song for you

It is a song of love.

I've come to dance a dance for you

I've come to dance a dance for you

I've come to dance a dance for you

It is dance of love.

The song enabled me to consciously connect to my womb centre, which in turn allowed me to feel my wounding, my joy, my enquiries, my rage, my love. I still from time to time take a walk to sing to my womb, I love the connection and the peace I experience from doing it.

Do you have a practice to connect you to your menstrual or female life cycle?

How do you think charting your menstrual cycle would help you in relation to your work, relationship, children and social aspects of your life?

If you are considering a practice, what would work well for you?

I use a wall chart for Molly, it is easy to note down e.g. her transition days, what day she starts her bleed, what days or phases she finds difficult. It's a quick and easy practice.

I prefer noting my moon cycle in my journal/diary. I like to record my energy levels, my emotions, when I am at my most creative, when I need to rest etc.

Experiment with works for you, ask your daughter what she does or if she'd like to try along with you. Involve your partner, let him or her know what you are doing and why. And let's not forget our son's, it's time to stop hiding our blood from them, it's time to educate us all in the potency, power and sacredness of our menstrual and female life cycle – oh yeeesssss!!!

For menstrual cycle resources contact Rachel Crowe at www.moontimes.co.uk

Embracing Becoming a Crone

Knowing now, why I (as a menopausal woman) experience certain physical and emotional symptoms is empowering, that knowledge has been transformational.

Menopause is all about transformation.

Not knowing this at that time of peri menopause, not knowing why I felt such rage or sadness, or anxiety was confusing because I was also feeling excitement, joy and liberation. I was fighting against the perceived 'negative' emotions of rage, sadness and anxiety.

In retrospect, I think I started my peri menopausal years when I was in my late forties, I was vaguely aware of *the change* but had no women around me who modelled or even spoke about how *beautifully* significant this phase of our lives can be.

I did try and raise the subject of menopause once when I was with friends for an evening. I was immediately shut down by the male in the group who aggressively told me he did not want to talk about the 'fucking menopause'. Stifled by being 'shut down' I did not pursue the conversation, I didn't seek out supportive books, or groups, I didn't even raise the subject again within female only company, and I didn't talk about it with Rob. Such was the disconnection and loss of my intuitive self.

Thank the goddess for the menopause! Yes, seriously, this phase in my life is the most wonderous, most potent most interesting, most magical time of my life. It is the last phase of my life so I am absolutely embracing it, the wisdom available to me now is mine for the taking. I have *gathered my bones*, I have reclaimed my Wild Woman, I have chosen to be a Wise Woman and it feels powerful, and juicy and just as it needs to be.

It is no accident that I now feel this way about becoming a Crone. I chose to do the work required of me, by me, to step over the threshold for the most important transition of my life. I chose to seek out the place I needed to be to heal. I chose to dive deep inside my Soul and face the shadows. And in doing so I have danced with my ancestors around fires, I have held my inner child and spoken softly to her, I have raged at my wounding and felt despair for the world.

Layers that had become too heavy to wear any longer were peeled off until I stood naked and saw myself for the first time as a wise, potent, empowered woman. The disintegration of all that I thought I was, all that I thought mattered, all that I thought I was afraid of, allowed me to open the door to my Soul.

I see, I know, I am so deeply connected to my intuition, I no longer accept the unacceptable, I no longer ask questions such as "*Am I good enough*", or in moments of doubt, I stop and remind myself that *"Yes I **am** good enough"* and I thank my shadow for the wisdom I learnt from her.

I'm not pretending the menopause hasn't also been challenging. It has. It is not just the spiritual, soulful and emotional shifts it is also the physical changes.

When I was young and peachy skinned, tight muscles and feeling oh so sexy, I claimed that *"I won't mind getting wrinkly and old"!*

For me, looking older came slowly, slowly, gently and then suddenly BAM there she was, an elder woman, looking back at me in the mirror. I was shocked, I pulled my skin taught across my brow and my chin. I lifted the fold of skin on my eyelid. My belly is unmistakably round and soft, I can grasp a handful of flesh. My bottom has become saggy and my breasts several sizes larger.

Clothes I had enjoyed wearing no longer feel comfortable. I can't bear tightness around my belly or my breasts. I need to feel unrestricted in my clothes, comfortable, but I still want to look great, to look sexy, to look attractive.

I used to love getting dressed up to go out for an evening, I was always confident in how I looked and enjoyed wearing clothes to express my sexuality and sensuality. I feel very differently about nights out now. I try on piece after piece of clothing, none of them feeling quite right, none of them looking how I want to look in them.

So, I am learning a new way of feeling good about how I look. I am learning to honour my new curves, to welcome my softness. I am beginning to enjoy now being seen as an elder woman!

Contrary to 'popular opinion' that elder women are not attractive or sexy or beautiful, I have the opinion that we are indeed all those things with bells on! When I look at my elder women friends, I instantly see their beauty. When I look at myself I still find it a little difficult to see my beauty. But that is changing and I have moments of loving the way I now look.

How about those hot flashes!?!

When I first started having them, I preferred to call them energy surges because for me that's what they were. Starting at my feet, I would feel an intense vibration as the energy moved all the way up through my body into my head, accompanied by heat. It was the most amazing Kundalini experience. These continued for about a year and a half, slowly changing over that period of time. Now, they really are hot flashes. The feeling has moved upward and starts now either in my womb or in my solar plexus and up into my head. I get REALLY red and hot and damp and have to strip off layers of clothing immediately, quickly, don't get in my way cause I'm burning! I am woken several times in the night from the heat, finding comfort in the cool spots of the bed, I throw the covers off me and simply pull them back again as the heat passes. I think of my hot flashes now as the shifting of energy which no longer serves me and the settling of a new vibration, cleared energy bringing me each time closer to my Crone Wisdom.

There was also a period when I experienced extreme tiredness, similar to that which I had during the first three months of pregnancy. I had learnt to honour the signals my body gave me by this stage. And so, when the tiredness dropped in, I rested. I would curl up on the sofa or take myself to bed. I would be clear to my family that I needed to have a quiet, uninterrupted half hour or so. Being clear, open, gentle, honest about what I need, what isn't helpful, what is difficult has been immensely supportive to us all. There is no second guessing by Rob, no coded messages from me and Molly has learnt along with us. If I have shut my bedroom door for a nap, I hear her saying "*Mumma Angie nap"* and she'll make a snoring sound as she walks by.

My final bleed was very long and for the first part, heavy, like it hadn't been since I'd been doing my healing work and not until I was 57 years old.

I was utterly exhausted. On the one hand, the longer the bleed went on the more concerned I became – because I was relating it to the Fibroid and something being 'wrong', illness and death.

On the other hand, my intuition was telling me this *was* my final bleed, my womb shedding what needed to go making space for the new.

So, although it certainly wasn't illness, it was most definitely death. But not my passing from this world, it was the death of my old self, making way for my Crone wisdom.

When I spoke with other womb wise women about what I was experiencing I felt re-assured, however, I did also feel like my life force energy was draining away from me with such intense blood loss. I contacted Jules as a trusted wise woman. She suggested I see my GP as the bleed had by that point been going on for a month. I knew this was sensible advice and so I went.

I was referred to hospital to have a Hysteroscopy, an examination to check the lining of the womb and the cervix. The examination is done with a tiny camera inserted into the vagina. A biopsy is also generally taken. I was very frightened when I went for the procedure.

Rob was with me and we sat silently waiting for my turn.

The nurses and Dr were wonderful, kind, compassionate, understanding, attentive and they really listened to me when I said how scared I was. One Nurse held my hand as the procedure started. It wasn't painful, it was uncomfortable. And it was horribly intrusive, the feeling of vulnerability and exposure never decreases each time I have to put my legs into the stirrups and part my legs for examinations.

I had a blood test too, to measure my FSH levels.

Several weeks later I received the result. My womb, cervix, ovaries and vagina were completely normal, my blood test showed I was post-menopausal. I was told that if I had any more bleeds, including spotting I should go back for another examination.

I was relieved with the results but didn't actually feel I *was* yet post-menopausal and I learnt that FSH level tests were often inaccurate. I have had several 'spotting's' since then and have chosen not to be examined again.

I see my acupuncturist every month, I feel healthy and intuitively I felt my womb still had a little more shedding to do.

And so, the heat waves continue, I know I'm better off not drinking coffee or wine and to stay off dairy foods in order to alleviate that symptom. I've learnt to moderate my diet, drink and eat more healthily than I have ever done (I also know there is *more* I can do but I don't beat myself up when I do have a coffee and a pastry!).

I am still enjoying my menopause years, still tuning in to my changed body (which I am continuing to love and honour), to my spiritual and emotional being, embracing each new day with such deep gratitude to the magnificence of womb wisdom.

Menopause is still though a taboo subject for many women and men. Attitudes are changing slowly, I have been aware of several radio talks over recent months, but sadly the conversations have largely focused on the perceived negative experiences and changes (hot flashes, mood swings, insomnia etc) and the goal is always to eliminate symptoms and always with HRT treatment or hysterectomy.

In the mainstream there is rarely any conversation about natural remedies such as herbs, diet, acupuncture, or spiritual practice such as meditation. Or how to tune in to the transformation, embrace the transformation, honour our changing body or how to reclaim our intuition and innate womb wisdom.

I want Molly to be supported to *'embrace and work with'* her Menopause experience, just as she is with her menstrual cycle. It is her right to be given alternatives to the mainstream views on menopause which responds with hormone replacement treatment or a hysterectomy.

I hope I will still be here when she reaches her menopause years. My peri menopause years were in my late forties, and the physical transitions not until I was in my mid/late fifties. I had my final bleed aged 57. So, I may not be here. I like to think I will and I'd love to be able to support Molly through her menopause years but if not me then other womb wise women.

I have written a couple of stories to support Molly with the phases of her menstrual cycle, here are two of them.

A Double Enchantress Day!

Warning! Warning! Laya and Molly were both in the Enchantress phase of their moon cycle – which meant they were both feeling that 'nitty gritty' energy. 'Nitty Gritty?' Yes! 'Nitty Gritty'. This means in some moments they felt irritable, or cross, or frustrated. And this meant that for Molly, on this particular day, she just felt like she needed to swear (using very rude words towards her very good friend Laya). Oh my. And this meant Laya got rather fed up and told Molly "Stop swearing at me Molly!". Well, the two Enchantress women managed to muddle and fuddle their way through the day. Sometimes laughing, sometimes grumpy, sometimes quiet and sometimes shrieking. The good thing is, both Molly and Laya knew they would soon move into the Crone phase of their moon cycle, and this meant they would feel calm and quiet and enjoy a dreamy time together.

A Dark Moon Day

It was the day of the Dark Moon and Angie and Molly had both started mooning. Molly was very pale and still and doing great big yawns. (Make a yawn sound).

Rob had made them both an energy booster smoothie for breakfast, delicious, 'thanks Rob'. Angie felt tired and needed to be still too, so they both decided to have a cup of tea and sit by the fire.

Molly was telling Angie how much she had enjoyed the night before with her friend Emma. Emma had come over to hang out with Molly, "Snuggles, mate" Molly told Angie.

A little later on after a few story's and listening to some music, Molly asked for a hot water bottle. "Bottle" she said as she rubbed her belly. Angie put the kettle on and Molly took herself off to her room. She slipped off her shoes and snuggled up under her duvet. Angie brought her the hot water bottle, kissed molly on her forehead and asked if she needed anything else.

"Nopety, nope, nope" said Molly and "Byeee",

191

which told Angie she just wanted some time and space to herself.

"See you later Moll's" said Angie as she left her room and pulled the door closed.

Brother Jake

So how is it to be a sibling of a disabled child? I think a fair bit about this, about what impact there has been on Jake as he grew up and when Rob and I are no longer here. Jake has a gentle, quiet wisdom, he is also a private man. He is steady, analytical and has an ability to take a broad view of things. I am so very grateful to my beautiful son Jake for his wisdoms and his analytical brain! He has often brought a perspective to a situation which my brain does not automatically go to in decision making.

When he was born, I felt such a deep love and connection to the universe through this little being. I instantly, completely, unconditionally loved my baby boy. For seven years he was an only child but he showed no jealously or displacement when Molly was born. He was very sweet with her, he loved making her laugh and cuddling up with her for bed time stories.

When I started writing this book, I thought I was

going to have a whole chapter with a focus on what it is to be a sibling of a disabled child. I spoke with Jake about this and asked if he would be willing to have a conversation with me to share his thoughts on this. His response was that he felt the subject requires a book in itself, not just a chapter in this one. He's right of course. So, I decided not to delve deeply into the subject for now. This book is purely from my perspective and I want to honour the fact that Jake is a private person and has made a valid and important point. So, I am sharing what I have observed and leaving the rest for (perhaps) another book.

I have no doubt that there have been situations over the years which have caused wounding to Jake. I know that there were times when I was not fully present as a mother, dealing with my pain and depletion. I know there were times when I intervened on his behalf to try and protect him from painful experiences, which may well have disempowered him. I am not admonishing myself for any mistakes I made, I know I always do the very best I can do and I am a good mother. As a wise woman, I simply want to acknowledge that as mothers, even when we try our very best to do the right thing for our children, we will sometimes get it wrong and there will be wounding.

Jake was very tolerant as a teenager. We had a house big enough to have his group of friends come over and a 'summer house' at the end of the garden where they had a space away from adults to hang out in private. Molly has always been a sociable being and so when Jake's friends were in the house, she wanted to join in. There is a 7-year gap between them, Jake at the age of 13 onwards didn't particularly want his 6-year-old sister hanging around. But she did hang out with him and his friends. I don't recall putting pressure on Jake to allow this, but that isn't to say I didn't. I also know that there was an individual in Jake's extended friendship group who used his 'disabled' sister as a weapon against him. This one particular boy was nasty to Jake. He overtly excluded him from group activities on occasions and was manipulative and a bully. He came with his own set of problems of course but my heckles were up when he was around.

Jake was also incredibly giving to Molly when he had girlfriends over and to stay. Molly was interested and drawn to his girlfriend's and wanted again to be included. Jake's first serious girlfriend also had a sibling with learning difficulties. Her brother was on the autistic spectrum and his parents had chosen a very different approach to education and social life opportunities. He went to

195

a residential special school and was only at home on weekends. Jake has told me he and his girlfriend were partly drawn to each other because they both had a disabled sibling and a common ground in what that meant to them. His girlfriend was very vibrant and beautiful and fun and I think interested in the (social model of disability) approach we had chosen in contrast to her own and her brothers experience.

When we moved to Wales, there was a point when Jake really wanted to come and build his home here with his new girlfriend at that time, it was a serious relationship and he was thinking of their future together. She though did not want to come. She felt that if they did, at some point they would become responsible for Molly.

The 'After I am gone bit'

And she wasn't wrong in thinking that. The reality is, that some point I will die, so will Rob.

We have discussed what will happen for Molly and Jake at this time on several occasions. Jake has expressed his willingness to be there for Molly; he said when we asked him *"Of course I will, she's my sister".* We have assured him that we do not expect him to do this just because they are siblings BUT we are relieved and deeply grateful that Jake will step into that role.

He has grown up seeing how and what we have fought for, created and implemented in order for Molly to have a life of inclusion, of belonging, of value. He has an innate sense of justice, a deep understanding of human rights and he is a kind, wise, loving man. I do not want him to do anything out of a sense of duty or obligation. I hope he will meet someone and fall in love again and perhaps have his own children because I know these are things he wants. And he and I both know that whoever that person is, will need to have an open loving heart and love Molly as well as loving Jake.

But there's no certainty in anything that we plan or wish for. We will have no control over the decisions made, we will have no control of responding to the current political and social conditions.

No control!

And accepting that, letting go of a need to control has been a massive piece of work for me.

I *am* planning for and hoping that whoever is around to love and care for Molly in addition to Jake, will pay careful attention to the wisdoms, experiences and outcomes I have worked hard to achieve in order for Molly to have a 'good life', a happy life, a life with friendship, a life of belonging, a life of participation and of value for who she is. And vitally, that Jake will also receive love and support throughout his life.

Practicalities

And how can that be accomplished beyond Jake? Rob and I have written a Will and we have instructed a Solicitor to arrange a Trust Fund and a Court of Protection for Molly's day to day finances. There are other specific practical issues that will need to be addressed. I sincerely wish that each practical issue will be dealt with from a place of love, with a deep understanding of the Social Model of Disability and without projection of any individuals personal shadows.

I am writing this at the beginning of 2019. We are all living at Spirals, our home since 2012 and as far as I know right now, will continue to be our home for a long time, possibly until Rob and I have died. And there is the possibility that Rob and/or I may reach an age when we are no longer able to care for Molly as we do now and another person/s will step in before we are dead.

I wish for Molly to stay in our family home, unless she expresses otherwise. She is comfortable here; she knows it well and is able to have a level of supported independence here that she did not previously experience and is unlikely to experience elsewhere, certainly not in a care home. So long as the gate to the lane is closed and someone is in ear-shot she is free to choose where she goes and when. This is massively important. Everyone's free will is vital to their wellbeing. Without our free will to make the choices we want to make we become restricted, frustrated, depressed, angry. Molly has a free spirit; it is who she is.

A Council of Aunties and Uncles

Molly is also a communicator and a teacher when people are willing to listen, to watch and to open themselves to a different way of communicating. She is emotionally intelligent and sensitive to other people's emotional state. She is happiest with people who understand when she needs her own space and when she wants company. She does not like people trying to coerce or manipulate her into doing something, who of us does?

Thankfully she can clearly demonstrate what she does not want to do. Timetables and fixed structures do not suit her, being with people who have a need to control or who think they know better than Molly what she wants have no place in Molly's life. It would be a road to frustration and conflict and I know from experience it would be Molly who would be blamed in such situations and labelled as *'aggressive', 'non-compliant', 'difficult'* when she would actually only be *saying "I don't want this"* and trying to set her own boundaries.

I hope that Rob and I will be around for a good while longer! The people who are in our and Molly's life now may well be totally different 10 –

20 years down the road. Jake may have a long-term partner, have his own children and moved away, up the road or half way around the world. Impossible to know!

So, as individuals and groups of friends come and go, I keep my eye on the ball, I talk to those whom I know Molly loves and they her, about how important it is that their input, their knowledge, their experience and wisdom is vital in supporting what happens after I am gone.

I had a conversation with a woman friend recently who told me she is exploring creating what she describes as 'A Council of Aunties'. This would be a group of women who know her and her daughter and who would make a commitment to provide support to her daughter in the event of the mother passing. Her idea really excited me, it is something I want to talk more about with her to explore the possibility of creating something for Molly, which would also support Jake.

The people involved will need to think outside the box, be creative, know how to listen, to observe and learn as the relationships develop.

While writing this piece Molly's one and only PA dropped out of the scene. I needed to find a solution, Molly was feeling bored and frustrated and missing having company other than me and Rob. So, what do parents of disabled adults do in these situations. Each time this has happened, and it has happened many times over the last 11 years, I have often felt despair. On this occasion however, Jake, Rob and I had a chat about what next. We talked through various ideas. Could we create a Group or Club with a focus on music, something Molly would enjoy, a place where she could meet other people, form friendships. Sounds great doesn't it? The reality though is that if we set it up as an Inclusive Group/Club, we would need to employ people as PA's. We would have a whole lot of beaurocracy, form filling, box ticking, fund raising to do. I did all of that in the early years. It was exhausting then; I have no desire to do it again now.

We then talked about going to Groups or Clubs further afield as there are none locally which Molly would enjoy. The problem with that is, they don't exist! Up to the age of 18 years we could probably find something but after that it's Day Centres or Respite or Specialist Groups.

Knowing What Works

And actually, Molly likes the things that go on in our community that aren't clubs or groups! There is a wonderful, vibrant and varied music scene here, Molly loves music. So, we came back to how does she access these things?

With a PA.

How do we find and recruit a PA or PA's who will be committed to the job?

There were two key issues to this, learnt from past experiences and re-evaluating how we use PA hours.

First of all, we know Molly does not want to go out every day, at the same time, to the same activity – that really is just a 'Day Centre' model in a different guise. What we do know for sure is that she needs and wants friendship, of course, her needs and wants are no different to yours or mine, she just interacts within them differently.

Secondly, in order to recruit and retain a really good PA who will support her to meet people and develop friendships, the hourly rate must reflect the responsibility and commitment required. Most people in 'care' work are paid extremely poorly. This is a serious issue. It makes no sense that people being employed to support people to participate in and contribute to our society, are so undervalued that their hourly rate of pay is usually minimum pay. We decided we would offer a significantly higher rate of pay. It means reducing the number of hours Molly has access to, but right now that is fine. She has clearly expressed she doesn't want a PA every day.

It felt good to reach this decision. I had thought that this transition was going to be so difficult, that thinking outside the box was going to bear no fruit this time. The fact that we sat as three heads, each bringing our own perspective, our collective experience, our knowledge of and our love for Molly enabled and empowered us to come to an easy and swift decision. And so, the search for new PA's started once again.

We have always invited applicants to come to our home for an informal interview and to see how she and Molly relate to one another. A problem has arisen from this. Molly see's the repetition of the process as a reflection of how the relationship has been with previous PA's. So, she has become stuck in her expectations of what they do together. This has largely been, in order of Molly's preference, snuggles, story's, café, bimble about town, gig, hanging out.

In truth, she is craving a close relationship and so snuggling is top of her list to the exclusion of everything else. Most PA's have been great at setting boundaries and Molly quickly understood them but sometimes struggled with not getting what she wanted and would become angry and frustrated.

It is also true that in most of her PA relationships, real friendship has developed and blossomed. It is true that some of the friendships fell away when the PA left her post, or when a PA has been dealing with life issues, and, as it is in anyone's life, some friendships do not last. Molly deals with the comings and goings of PA's and friendships far better than me! I am still learning to not feel like the world has ended when a PA leaves her post or when a friendship comes to a natural ending.

I know this is partly due to the overwhelming feeling of responsibility I have carried for creating and facilitating social opportunities for Molly. I am learning to let go of this.

Molly actually does not need me to form the *friendships* for her. She does this very well herself! She has always been a social being and has always drawn people to her.

I do of course have a responsibility to keep her safe and therefore I *am* involved in with who and when and where she goes. Finding a balance of supporting safe, independent friendship and not restricting her development and experiences in life can be challenging.

It is good to remind myself that Molly has had and continues to have wonderful friendships. Just as it is for all of us, she has experienced sadness as well as joy, frustration as well as fulfilment, boredom as well as excitement.

<u>Physical Health and Wellbeing</u>

Health is another really important aspect to look at for Molly's future wellbeing. This one freaks me out a bit. Molly is able to communicate if something hurts by saying "*ouch*" or *"hurt".* But she isn't able to be specific. She cannot say *"My tooth on the left at the back is aching" or "It stings when I wee"* or *"My throat is sore and it's hard to swallow".*

She was recently experiencing such discomfort/ pain in a tooth that she was unable to eat. Molly loves her food, so not eating was a sign that something was really painful. Naturally we asked her to open her mouth so we could take a look, 'absolutely not' was her response. She refuses to open her mouth for the dentist, I don't blame her. It's such an intrusive thing having teeth examined. When Molly was about 5 years old, she had some tooth decay and needed a filling and a tooth removal. This had to be done under General

Anaesthetic in the dental hospital. It was traumatic for us all. When she woke from the procedure, she was furious and in pain. She pulled the cotton balls stopping the bleeding out of her mouth and was very distressed. Ever since she unsurprisingly objects to any sort of examine of her mouth.

And then Rob had a brilliant, simple and effective solution to looking in her mouth. When she was snuggling into bed, so lying down, he began to make jokes which he knew would make her laugh. As she laughed, he quickly took a photo of the inside of her mouth. It worked. He managed to get several photos of her teeth without any stress involved for anyone! The dentist was then able to literally get a 'snap shot' of the condition of her teeth. At this point he felt it would be appropriate to refer her to the dental hospital for a check-up, not under GA but with sedation. My body contracted with anxiety.

I decided to contact my Homeopath who had successfully treated me with a Mercury Detox (I have a mouth full of Mercury fillings). She did the usual thorough consult and prescribed Molly a course of Tissue Salt remedies to strengthen her teeth. She has been taking them for a couple of months now and has not had any repeat of the pain she previously experienced several times. Both of my children grew up with very little illness and both only ever had anti biotics in emergencies. Jake had an infection in his knee and was rushed into hospital, where he stayed for about 8 days and was given intravenous anti biotics. Molly got peri-orbital cellulitis and too was rushed to hospital and given a course of anti-biotics. Apart from those lifesaving situations I had always used natural remedies and allowed them to heal with their body's own resources, love and rest. Jake is now an adult and makes his own choices about how he treats illness. Molly will always be dependent on others to address health issues. I ask that whoever that is after I am gone, after Rob has gone, that Molly continues to receive natural medicines whenever possible. I am not negating the fact that numerous lives are saved and recovery aided using western medicines, procedures and skills. But I believe it is also critical to know, it does too have limitations and can in some situations be detrimental to health, wellbeing and healing. I want Molly's health to be approached and viewed holistically i.e. her physical, mental, spiritual and emotional health.

She is a really healthy person. On the rare occasion she has a cold or sore throat she moves through the stages of those infections with ease. She rests, she drinks plenty of liquid, wholesome food, allows the fever to run its course and she's back to full vitality within days. This type of information is critical for the wellbeing of someone who cannot communicate for themselves.

The Mental Capacity Act would allow the local authority to make decisions on her behalf based on what *they* think is best for her, when they do not *know* her, so again I reiterate, the importance of having information to share, a circle or council of people who love her can support her in being where she wants to be, with who she wants to be and how her health and wellbeing is addressed.

For example. It will not be possible to give Molly a Smear test or a Mammogram (I have had both myself in the past but in recent years have made the choice not to have any more. Both are controversial with growing evidence that mammograms are harmful and smear tests unreliable). Molly cannot consent to procedures or investigations and would not understand what was being done. To do either would be an abuse. There is an alternative to mammograms, called a thermogram. At present this can only be done privately – exactly the sort of cost which could be covered from her Trust fund.

Having a Social Life

And of course, her social life opportunities and experiences are critical to her wellbeing. Finding social activities for Molly was often challenging. When Jake had expressed an interest in doing something, e.g. Ice Hockey, it was simple. We found out where the ice rink was, what days the ice hockey club ran, what he needed to wear, how much it cost and enrolled him. No questions asked.

With Molly it was different. Mainstream clubs would not accept her without support, but they didn't provide support, there was no funding for support, so she could not attend. When the SEN and Disability Act came into being this was not actually lawful. However, the discrimination continued. In my work, I was constantly being told by parents that their child was being prevented from joining after school clubs or social clubs or if they had managed to get them in, they were then excluded because there was no support in the setting and the staff were unable or unwilling to differentiate their practice.

In order for children and young people, who need additional support to be included, to have opportunities for play, socialisation, varied experience, it is often necessary for Warrior parents and ally's to either fight a huge and painful battle to get their child into a provision that doesn't want them there or create something inclusive themselves.

When Molly was about 7 years old my dear friend Jo Cameron told me, that a long established and successful inclusive theatre group were coming to Brixton to support those interested in creating the same in our borough. Within a year we had our own inclusive theatre group up and running, providing opportunities for children age seven to eighteen to explore the dramatic arts.

I was involved from the beginning as a committee member and as a trainer to the volunteers and paid group leaders. Every person involved in supporting the inclusive theatre group received inclusion training, including up to date legal requirements as well as social model practice.

Molly loved going every week. She flourished in such a welcoming and inclusive environment. The young woman who was employed as the project leader remains a very good friend. Fran was innovative, inclusive, enthusiastic, open, a great communicator with the young people, the volunteers, the committee and the parents.

An example of her skills was in one end of term play in which she created a theatre happening in

211

the round. There were several different scenes, each interconnected but acted separately around the room. The audience moved from scene to scene, in any direction they wished. Molly was cast as The Ghost. This meant she was able to move in and out of each scene as she chose, the other characters in each scene would then react to her presence as and when she appeared. It was perfect. Simple. Imaginative. Inclusive.

Molly attended for many years. When she was eleven, just before she left primary school, a new group leader started and for us it all fell apart.

The group leader instructed one of the volunteers to physically hold Molly to prevent her freedom of movement during the rehearsals and performance.

A friend of Molly's told me; the group leader would shout "*Hold her! Hold her!*".

When I saw the performance, I was horrified by how Molly was treated. I could not beleive I was watching my daughter being restrained in an inclusive theatre performance! I wanted to run onto the stage and pull the volunteer away from Molly. I felt like all the years of helping to create and facilitate an Inclusive opportunity for Molly and all the disabled children in the borough was being sucked into a deep, dark hole.

Fortunately, Molly's strength of will was such that she managed to struggle free from the grip of the adult holding her to a huge cheer from the audience.

In the following days a massive row ensued and I decided to leave my role as Chair of the Committee and remove Molly from the theatre group. It was one battle too many too fight at that point in my life.

Thankfully, we happened to reconnect to an old friend who was volunteering at another inclusive theatre group in a borough nearby, which we had not known existed. And so, Molly started there, staying until she was seventeen and we moved to Wales.

This was a wholly positive experience for her, for us and for the theatre group. The group leaders were wonderful and created fabulous performances enabling all the children and young people to participate in meaningful ways.

The last performance before we left London included a song from West Side Story. Molly had been practicing at home and we were looking forward to the performance. All the young people came out onto the stage and stood facing the

213

audience. Molly walked over to the edge of the stage and sat down, facing the audience. The music began, everyone started singing, including Molly, whose voice range out with sheer delight. She sang the song along with her fellow performers, choosing to be in her own space to do it but still with and a part of the whole. Rob and I sat in the audience with tears of joy streaming down our faces.

Have a go, see what works and what doesn't.

There were many activities Molly participated in over the years, some worked well, others didn't – just as it is for any child.

There was a wonderful Circus Skills Club every Saturday in Brixton. Molly enjoyed going and had a go with most things, including the unicycle. It was actually a very naturally inclusive club, no additional support staff asked for or required.

When we were Home Edding a group of us would sometimes go swimming or to the local ice rink. Molly was familiar with the ice rink as Jake played in the Streatham team and we were there at least twice a week for practice. Molly liked skating for a short time but it felt very unsteady to her and rather restrictive as she needed to hold onto someone all the time.

We discovered a cycling session, specifically for disabled people to access a whole range of bikes. The session was every Friday held in Brockwell Park, just a short walk from where we lived. Once Molly had her PA's in place, she was able to go along with her mate and take part in the session. She loved it. There were side by side bikes which she could control, bikes she could sit in the front of and be wheeled around the track, regular bikes she could try out.

The people who ran the group were delightful, they were welcoming, fun and had no problem when Molly cycled anti clockwise around the track! She met Betty there, who was a volunteer and we discovered was also our neighbour! Betty was gorgeous, she became a good friend to us all. She asked Molly if she'd like to learn to ride a regular bike, and once a week we would meet her in the park for a lesson. It was incredible, within weeks Betty had supported and taught Molly so well that she had the confidence to mount, pedal and ride a bike a short distance with Betty just holding the back. She also invited Molly to her workshop, where she recycled old bicycle tyres into all sorts of things, to help out in whatever way Molly wanted, usually hanging out and chatting.

What I have learnt throughout the years is to let

go of my perception of what a social life and friendship is. For a very long time I projected my own desires, needs or aspirations around what friendship is onto Molly and when I witnessed how she had a different experience to that which I knew, I felt she was missing out or being excluded when actually (for the most part) she wasn't. Molly has her own way of being in relationship with others, her own way of interacting in social situations, which give her great joy and satisfaction. To understand, accept and embrace these differences has empowered and enabled me to relax, to know I do not need to control or fix situations.

Molly is very able to communicate when she is feeling safe and enjoying a situation and when she feels overwhelmed and anxious. By clearing my projections, I am much better equipped to hear and see what is truly going on for her and respond accordingly.

For some time now Molly has chosen to go and sit in our car, with her iPod and speaker and listen to her music. She will stay there for hours sometimes, every so often coming into the house to go to the loo, or ask for a drink or food, occasionally to have a stroll and also to hang out with whoever is around. It took me a long time to accept that this was OK. I would try and persuade her to do something else (something I thought was of more value or more interesting). I even stopped her from going in the car on occasions believing I could manipulate her into losing interest in it. Of course, she found that very upsetting, she was understandably angry with me for preventing her doing the very thing she enjoyed. I realised I was projecting my own stuff about social interaction on her and creating a problem that didn't actually exist other than in my own mind.

Interestingly I have met two other parents whose child also enjoys sitting in their family car. One parent was completely at ease with it and recognised that it was important for his child. The other parent found it extremely challenging and, just as I had done, was creating anxiety for himself and his child by objecting to it.

I recognise now that her sitting in the car is actually like a daily practice of meditation. It is her choice to sit in the car to listen to her music, to be alone, unbothered. Her space. Her time. Her choice. Her ability to *know* she needs her space and to then *create* it in a way which works for her, with free will and to derive pleasure from it is a truly remarkable teaching.

217

Remember the Gifts!

When we moved to Wales, we were determined to find activities and groups where Molly would have the opportunity to meet people and develop friendships if she so wished. We felt we needed to be open to everything, to not restrict opportunity because of past experiences. In the first instance, before we got to know people, this boiled down to trying out a specialist service group. We had already met with a Social Worker in order to apply for Direct Payments to gain access to PA's again. This wouldn't happen immediately, so in the mean time we asked the social worker what else was available. He signposted us to a fairly local group and arranged for us to meet with another social worker to take a look. Rob and I both intuitively knew this was not a good idea but we were desperate to find something for Molly, never a great place to make decisions from, and so we put on our usual 'upbeat enthusiastic parent' mask and set off to the group.

The welcome was nice enough and when we went in there was a small group of young people chatting and laughing, having a cup of tea. First impressions were positive. Molly appeared to feel comfortable and began to have a look around, going from one room to another to see what was

218

what. I was having a really nice conversation with the social worker who had met us there, it was all going well.

About 10 minutes in, the group leader approached me. She came straight out with *"I don't think we can support Molly here. This group isn't right for her"*. I was stunned and furious. She hadn't introduced herself. She hadn't had any interaction with Molly. She'd not introduced herself to Molly, not welcomed her, nothing, and YET she decided after 10 minutes my daughter didn't fit in.

I burst into tears and left the building; I didn't want Molly to see how upset I was. The social worker and Rob followed me out. I wanted to leave immediately, however the social worker asked if we would stay and have a conversation with the group leader. She joined us outside and we all sat at a table. I was too angry and upset to speak, I just couldn't connect to my Inclusion Warrior.

Rob was brilliant, he took control of the situation and explained to the group leader that what she had said was inappropriate and how hurtful it is for parents to be spoken to about their child in the way she had. She reiterated her view that they could not support Molly, that they didn't have the resources. I could have swung for her. We had put all this crap behind us when we left the school system. We hadn't listened to our instinct or to our intuition. We had ignored our years of experience and wisdom.

Fortunately, Molly had seen enough of the group and had made her way out to leave anyway, she was very happy to get back into the car and go home. She never mentioned it or asked to go again.

As we began to settle and meet people, someone mentioned a gathering that happened the first Monday of every month. They described it as a music improvisation. I found out the name of the woman who hosted it and decided to call her to get a sense of her approach and attitude in relation to inclusion. I called Maggie and had a most wonderful conversation with her. I didn't say *"My daughter has learning difficulties".* I wasn't going to label her again. I asked Maggie if it was OK for people to come and express themselves in their own way, she *said "YES! This is what it's all about".* I said my daughter has her own way of communicating, she said *"I get it, I communicate differently too".* And so, the conversation went on. It was such a joy, she clearly did 'get it' and was really enthusiastic about us going there. And we did.

Maggie's Barn is a gem. Everyone is welcoming.

It is a place where people can truly express themselves, Unbound and authentic.

On our first visit we felt we had struck gold. Molly climbed the steps up into the vast attic and took in the space. There were instruments, chairs and settees, a fire and a number of people playing instruments, or drawing, or chatting. Maggie was at her keyboard and her elderly mother was sat on the opposite side of the room. Molly sat down too and watched Maggie, who then started to make wonderful vocal sounds, not singing, but sounds of the Soul. From across the room, Maggie's mother began to reply to the sounds with her own Soulful vocals, creating a beautiful conversation between them. I could see Molly's face light up, she smiled broadly, she started to move her body and then join in the conversation with *her* own sounds. Her face shone with an expression of *'At last I've found people who speak my language'*.

Molly has continued to go to Maggie's Barn on and off since we've been here. In the first couple of years she and Rob went regularly and took part in several of the Cabaret nights and a performance at The Small World Theatre (a fantastic venue in Cardigan). I was so excited to go and see Molly in her element, doing her own thing, being valued and included in a totally natural, organic way.

The first time she performed at Maggie's was at the summer Cabaret. Several acts had done their thing and then Maggie sat at her keyboards, Rob took his place with his guitar, Pete with his saxophone and another musician joined them. Maggie asked Molly if she'd like to come up and join them. Molly took off her shoes and walked to the stool behind the microphone. She sat down and crossed her legs, taking the mic from its stand. Maggie started to play some chords and Molly immediately began rapping. Taking cues from Molly, the other musicians joined in. They were all looking to Molly for the pace and rhythm. She was incredible! Her confidence and skill just blew me away. Occasionally, she glanced behind herself to acknowledge the musicians and take note of what they were doing in relation to what she was doing, they were all playing as one! It was one of the most wonderful, uplifting moments ever in Molly's and our lives.

One of the many beautiful aspects of living here is that once you find your tribe there is a thread that runs through. One person knows another and slowly but surely the sense of belonging grows. Even when the tribe doesn't see each other often, especially over the winter months as we all tend to hibernate, as soon as the gigs, or events start up again everyone is there.

The venues are perfect for Molly, small, safe, accessible and extremely welcoming. And many people in our community know her and look out for her, dance with her, chat with her. This just wasn't possible in London. Here it is a breeze, it's fun and relaxing. Although Rob and I still need to keep our eyes on where Molly is, we also know others are too and there are no barriers, physical or attitudinal. Molly is empowered to make her own choices while she's there. Just like Wingford Rd, this is a very inclusive community.

And, there *are* still blocks and restrictions to her having company when she wants it. She will always need others to support her inclusion and participation in life. My aim now is, as it has always been, to facilitate a community who will include and value her without me having to instigate it.

Society often assumes that people who require assistance do not have anything of value to *offer*, hence the terms like 'service user'.

This could not be further from the truth. It has never only been about what others have to offer Molly; it is also very much about what she has to offer them.

Over the years, PA's, friends and family, have spoken of the value and importance Molly's friendship is to them. For some, within the friendship they have discovered a new level of confidence, for many it is the expression of joy and laughter she initiates. For all, it is her ability to show us how to be unafraid to express ourselves – she does this with brilliant confidence and self-assuredness.

Therefore, I know that when we shift people's perceptions, when we empower people to understand what disability is and what it isn't, when we have a situation in which others will instigate and invite relationship with people who are otherwise isolated or ignored, then we will have an inclusive society.

This poem by Suzi (originally a PA and now a friend) is a beautiful expression of their friendship.

<u>*Miss Molly Molly Moo*</u>

Miss Molly Molly Moo,

I love hanging out with you!

Even when it's raining, we still find things to do.

Miss Molly Molly Moo

Our days are so content,

Milkshakes, walks and snuggles,

And stories of where we went.

Miss Molly Molly Moo,

You always make me smile,

Shivers and quivers and fallings over -

Your own unique style!

Miss Molly Molly Moo,

Thanks for a lovely time

I can't wait for our next adventure

Dearest friend of mine.

I chose to share the following story too, as it beautifully demonstrates how well a PA can support creating community. Laya introduced Molly to a number of her friends over the years she worked for her. Molly loves catching up with them each year at Unearthed festival.

<u>A Visit to Tilly and Ava by Laya 2015</u>

On Monday, Laya and Molly went to visit Tillybug and Avababy. Molly enjoyed the journey to little

Newport as she was excited about seeing her new friends. When they arrived, everyone had a hug and started chatting and catching up on each other's news. Molly was looking at Avababy, she was reminded of two brilliant jokes she had learnt and loved telling. So, Molly asked Tilly and Laya

"Which B drinks the most milk?".

"We don't know Molly; which B does drink the most milk?" replied Tilly and Laya smiling.

Molly smiled back at them and said "A baby!". Everyone burst out laughing, "That's a great joke Molly" giggled Laya.

Then Molly asked "Which B produces the most milk?" Laya and Tilly looked at each other but couldn't think what the answer was.

"A boo Bee" Molly said and they all burst out laughing again.

"What brilliant jokes" Laya chuckled.

Tilly saw Molly looking at Avababy, "Would you like to hold her?" she asked

"Yeah, yeah, yeah" Molly whispered.

So, Tilly gently laid Ava in Molly's arms. Molly was delighted and held Ava very carefully and lovingly.

Laya took some photos of Molly and Ava and said "You're part of the family Molly".

"Yeah" thought Molly "I'm Mumma Molly".

Angie Northwood

Growing Our Community

We came to Wales for many reasons, buying the type of property we have was always with the idea in mind that other people could live here. A micro community was how I thought of it.

At this moment in time of writing we do have exactly that. Our dear neighbour Mara, who lives at the end of the track, has become a close friend. During the weeks when I was feeling very low without any PA support, Molly and I and Mara would go for walks every day, share meals and have a lazy few hours over a cup of tea, cake and Mara's exquisite storytelling and singing.

And then during that summer we had some old friends who came to stay in the Cottage. During the visit their daughter remarked to them how happy and relaxed they were, something they had not felt in a while. That evening as we sat out chatting late into the night, they were expressing how much they disliked where they currently lived and how much better they were feeling here, I asked *"Why don't you move here?"* *"Yes!"* they replied*, "we have actually been seriously thinking about that today, we were looking at properties to rent!"*

It was also the case that Mara was due to be spending 6 months over in California and she was getting desperate about finding someone to rent her house. So, the wheel was set in motion. I spoke to Mara, she spoke with our friends and as Mara left, Lee and Tracy and their daughter Grace moved in.

For the first few months Tracy did some PA hours for Molly. They got on great but Molly was right back in the same situation as before and the hours became tense for both Molly and Tracy. What worked better was when we all just got together socially, there was no pressure or expectations from or on anyone. Tracy found the courage to tell me the PA hours weren't working and we called it a day. Not without my usual distress, I thought we had found a solution but I had been hasty and rushed straight back into what I already understood was done and dusted. Molly and Tracy are now wonderful friend's in a natural and organic way, just as friendships are. Molly also has a wonderful friendship with Grace and with Lee.

Now, Lee lives here at Spirals and Tracy and Grace live just ten minutes away. Mara is back from her travels and is staying in the valley. Jake decided to move from London in 2016 and also lives with us. I LOVE having all my family in our nest!

We really do have our own little micro community. Molly greets Lee each evening when he gets back from work, Grace hangs out after school and over the weekends, we all get together for day trips, tea, lunch or evening parties. Molly has the freedom to move between our house and the Cottage as and when she chooses. Or she can ask to go and have a visit up at Mara's. It's wonderful for each and every one of us.

In the future, I can't know for sure, but I envisage, dream into, plan, for more in our micro community. Our home is big enough to reconfigure it to accommodate others, as and when it's needed. We have options, we made the choices we made in order to have these options. Right now, I feel excited about growing our community.

A Perfectly Splendid Day

It was a beautifully hot, sunny day again. At lunch time, Angie and Molly wondered up to see Tracy

231

and Grace. They had planned to go to Pizza Tipi later on but it was not going to be open after all. Angie and Tracy chatted about what they could all do instead. Molly and Grace were ready to go out right then, they were ready for an adventure!

So, they all agreed a walk in Henllan Woods along the river would be just fine. Rob drove the car up to Tracy's house, Barley dog in the boot, Grace and Molly and Tracy got in the back seats, Angie in the front with Rob and 'whoooosh' they were off. The journey only took five minutes, so quick as a flash they were out of the car and heading off into the woods. While they walked, they all chatted and laughed, especially each time one of them tripped or stumbled on the tree roots. This gave Molly an idea. She started playing the 'push Tracy in the bush' game, a favourite game they play whenever they go for a walk which makes them both hysterical!

The Molly suggested a game of hide and seek, so off Angie and Grace ran to hide behind a huge old oak tree. Barely though this was great fun and chased after them, barking and giving away where they were hiding. But it didn't really matter because Molly and Tracy weren't even looking for them, they just walked on by, what 'Cheeks McGee' they are.

Once they reached the meadow, they made their way across, turned around and headed back to the car. On the return walk, Grace asked Angie to play 'The Interview' game. While Angie and Grace asked each other questions, Rob and Molly has their own Interview game.

Rob asked Molly,

"What is your favourite music?"

"Marley" answered Molly

"What is your favourite food?"

"Cake" grinned Molly

"Do you like boots or pumps"

"Boots" replied Molly

"Where do you like to walk, town?"

"Nope" said Molly

"The beach?"

"Nope"

"Woods?"

"Nope" laughed Molly

By this time, they had arrived back at the car. But this was not the end of their adventures. A quick trip to the shops for provisions as they were all gathering at Molly's house later that day for food, fun and laughter. Jenny and Nev and Pimple were coming too. Another tale to be told…

Me and Rob - Where We Are Now

We have been together since October 1985. We have had and continue to have a wonderful life together. Rob was just turning 21 when we met, I was 24. So, of course, we have changed a great deal since then. And, our life together has not always been easy, we have not always been happy together – or more precisely, we have not always been happy with ourselves and therefore not with each other. I can pin point the various stages in our relationship when we were dissatisfied with our life and unable to look beyond the obvious. We would look to work, lack of time together, lack of money, lack of something or other as the reason for our dissatisfaction. This was our perception.

I am using 'we' in this piece because, thankfully, we have both done our inner work (still doing our inner work) and spend time and space together to talk about the journey we have each taken to reach this phase in our lives when we are at ease within our relationship in a way that is different now we are elders.

By that I mean that both of us takes responsibility for what we feel and for the choices we make in response. We do not look to the other to fix that which needs fixing for ourselves. We know we can ask each other for support, space, to talk, to be heard without needing to be healed by the other. This is both empowering and powerful. We have both learnt to hold space for the other, to listen deeply and from a place of love and compassion.

It was not always like this. By the time we reached Wales our relationship was in crisis, which I have described in previous pages. There were two distinct moments when we concluded our relationship had reached its end. The first was after several years of being here, we had a big row, we have rarely rowed over our 33 years together. This was a humdinger.

Rob was burying his head in the sand about the need for his own healing journey and as a consequence he blamed me for his unhappiness and the state of our relationship. I on the other hand was a long way down the path on my journey and as a consequence knew it was a matter of healing, not blame. He projected a verbal pile of poop at me and I saw red. I turned myself from him and screamed from the deepest place of my Soul, I let lose my ancestral anger and pain, I was in that moment, a burning woman running from the flames. I was not going to be admonished, blamed or diminished for being a potent, wild woman.

Once I stopped my screaming, I gathered myself into action. I created my own space to be in, a nest in which to nurture myself, a safe haven, I could not bear to be in Rob's energy any longer. It was toxic for both of us. I set clear boundaries and took some time to reflect on what I needed to do next.

I was still sitting in Circle each month and so had a place of wisdom and nourishment in which to explore the very particular type of sadness I was feeling. I loved Rob but I knew without doubt that we could not continue in the way we were with each other. I had learnt to speak my Truth, not to blame, not to project and knew what my triggers were and how to respond to them. I told Rob that unless he was prepared to do *his* work, it was over. It wasn't fair on either of us to be in a relationship in which we could not be who we truly are and have what we truly wanted. I was no longer prepared to be anything but myself, I would not hide my anger, I would not be *'sugar and spice and all things nice'*. I would not own what was not mine. We could not continue as we were. I was prepared to call it a day, we were done if he did not step up and do his work.

And so, Rob started to do his work. He chose to see a counsellor and stepped onto his path of healing. Things slowly began to change and life became easier but there was still an undercurrent of dissatisfaction. Rob still wanted me to complete him, still looked to me for his happiness, and because I could not provide that for him, he felt abandoned by me. He kept telling me he loved me but I saw no evidence of this, I did not feel it energetically, the words sounded hollow and inauthentic.

During one of many conversations about the state of our relationship and what we were going to do, I told Rob his words did not ring true to me. He didn't understand when I explained that what he said sounded like a plea for me to make him feel better. And, so it went on.

The deeper the diving I did, the more I changed and the more he felt rejected.

One afternoon after yet another discussion about what he wanted from me; I came to the conclusion we really were done. I told Rob we were going around and around in circles and if he was so unhappy with me then he deserved to be with someone he did feel happy with. I cried as I said this, I told Rob it broke my heart to think we would not be together as elders. And, so we agreed it was time to go our separate ways.

Interestingly, on the very same day a couple who were living on our land at the time, were having the 'same' conversation. Rob and I then found ourselves responding to their situation. She had just had their second baby and was obviously devastated when her partner told her he was leaving. He moved out. Rob and I became surrogate grandparents and all our attention was focused on giving what we could manage to supporting her and her two beautiful children.

We learnt a great deal during this phase of our lives. We recognised a mirror had been held up to us. Rob began to notice how certain behaviours were no longer serving him, slowly but surely his heart opened and he began to peel back his layers, dive deep, let go of what needed to go and invite in the changes.

Spirals of Wellbeing – the land - was holding us all as we each tended to our wounds.

I was aware that as Rob worked through what he

wanted to let go of and invite in the new, he may have decided he no longer wanted to be with me! But what actually happened was that we were able to sit down together, while he expressed his wounding, I was able to listen without feeling threatened. He was able to show and express his vulnerability. Slowly and gently we found ways of being with each other. Our relationship is very different now. It is one in which we have both healed, transformed and still want to be together!

So, at this time of writing (2019), we are happy in our relationship because we are happy in ourselves. We are no longer fearful to express what we feel when we hit a block or are triggered. We honour the path we have journeyed together. We enjoy our life together. Each day we are filled with joy from the land we live in, from our home we have created together, from the work we each do and from our two beautiful children, who we are blessed to have living with us. We are both deeply grateful for the life we live and that we live it with love, still together.

Take Off Your Armour and Have a Cup of Tea

We often don't realise how much we have been holding on, until we begin to let go! How much we protect ourselves with barriers in order to survive, but in doing so, we get lost from ourselves, we become unable to reach out, unable to express our vulnerability and therefore unable to receive help, even in the times we most need it. So, more than anything else, creating your own space and time is of the utmost importance. A space and time to be creative, to dance, to sing, to write, play a guitar, shake a rattle, drum a drum. And to nurture and nourish yourself with rest (especially if you are menopausal, pregnant or menstruating) learn to stop, to listen, to breath, take a walk, be in nature, have a massage. Remind yourself to have fun, go out with friends, play, laugh. We always have a choice.

Making conscious choices, congruent to who we are at Soul level, is both empowering and potent, it is a vital piece of the process of transformation to becoming whole, becoming your beautiful *Wild, Wise* self.

When I qualified as a Soul Realignment practitioner, I chose to do a reading for myself. It was a life changing choice. I learnt who I am at Soul level, what the 'essence of me' is. It is all about communication, and creating community with compassion!

When I learnt this, I felt it in my body, my mind, my spirit, my Soul and realised, I did of course already know this! I started to consciously make my choices in alignment to who I am at Soul level.

Each congruent choice opens me to the flow of life force energy and the more life force energy I receive the more I am able to manifest what I truly want in life.

I offered Rob a reading, which he accepted. He too uses his reading to 'check in' with the choices he makes.

We both now set intentions aligned to who we are at Soul level and it has made a huge and positive difference to our relationship.

I used to get frustrated that Rob was 'always on the go', doing things, not stopping. But once I knew that who he is at Soul level is all about physical manifestation, I understood his need to be physical and to create tangible things. For him too, it was re-affirming, it made sense and it actually encouraged him to shift his focus into consciously creating space and time to do the things he really loves, to create space and time to making and building. Rob has learnt too in relation to my essence; he now understands that I am *not* drawn to physical exercise in the way he is and he no longer tries to encourage me to work out or stretch as a daily practice in the way that he does!

A practice I *do* use, is to start my day by tuning in to what I am feeling, both in my body and spiritually. As I wake up, I take a few moments to ask myself *"What am I feeling?" Excited? Anxious? Fearful? Joyful?*

"What is my body asking me to listen to?" Is my back aching? Do I have a headache? Do I feel energetic? Do I want to leap out of bed?

How I respond to these questions shapes my day. If I am feeling fearful and my back aches, I pretty much know there is an issue I need to talk about with someone, probably with Rob. If I choose to talk about it, to ask for us to sit down and communicate I am opening a channel to resolve what needs resolving, or explore what needs exploring, I also open myself to receive support if I ask for it.

In my early days of menopause, I negotiated getting some rest time, or having a back massage. I take a walk and give myself space and time to think through an issue, loosen up my body, breath, connect to the earth. I may choose to do some chakra singing, or a meditation or put on some music and dance. The choices are endless. Each one strengthens my path of living a life with love and gratitude – which quite simply brings me such deep joy and happiness.

Or

I could choose to keep it all to myself, be angry with whoever is around me, carry on regardless, put on my armour and pretend I am only strong, I am OK, I can do this alone. Be busy to distract, be busy to hide my vulnerability. I know from experience this leads ALWAYS to depletion, to depression, to disconnection to my Soul, to my intuition, disconnection to my *Wild Wise* self.

My 'old' voice would have said

"Time and space would be great, but I don't have any!"

"It's alright for you to talk!"

"But no one listens to me"

"I can't just stop, I'm too busy"

"I wish I could have time to myself but I have so much that needs doing"

And on and on and on………….

We are often afraid to ask for what we want for fear of rejection or upsetting someone. Afraid we will be seen as difficult, or demanding, or needy, or incapable, or not very nice. Afraid that if we reveal these aspects of ourselves, which we have been told are unacceptable, we will be exiled from our relationships. We have been taught that girls are '*sugar and spice and all things nice*', that it is our role to please others, to always be nice and kind and loving, to always put others before ourselves. So, it's little wonder that we struggle to consciously create space and time for ourselves, that we feel guilty, secretly wishing we could have a massage, go for a walk alone, rest, dance, simply because the urge takes us to dance. Men too struggle to ask for help, they have been taught that men must be tough, if they dare to show vulnerability they are told to '*man up*'. The patriarchy has damaged us all.

It is also true that by claiming our children, our work, our partners or our family prevent us from doing what we want, we diminish our responsibility, we blame others, situations, life itself. We use our busyness as a distraction. Because when we stop, when we close our computer, when we switch off the television, when we don't have just one more glass/bottle of wine we become aware of our-self. We *feel* what our body is telling us, we *feel* our emotions, we *feel* our pain, our fear, our stuckness. And we have a choice. Turn the telly back on, have another drink, stay on FB hour after hour, stay late at the office and ignore what your Soul is crying out for. OR seek a path of healing, in whatever way is right for you. Know it takes time and responsibility. It feels in equal measure, uncomfortable, scary, overwhelming, exhausting *and* exciting, joyful, calming, grounding and energising. When we clear space for ourselves we are giving ourselves the gift of nurture and nourishment. We must learn to become adept at knowing. Knowing when to rest, when to play, when to be busy, when we are most creative, when we least tolerate bullshit, when we are most able to speak our Truth.

"Women who try to make their deeper feelings invisible are deadening themselves. The fire goes out. It is a painful form of suspended animation"

Clarissa Pinkola Estes.

I denied myself space and time for years, claiming I was too busy, too much needed to be done, no one else will do it, only I can do it and on and on and on.

I believed those statements to be true. My barriers were so high, so thick, my armour so securely fitted I could hardly breath. My body gave me clear signs I needed to change what and how I was living my life, on many occasions. A frozen left shoulder – steroids and on I went. Depression – counselling, an opening but no real changes to my life patterns, on I went. Anxiety, breathlessness, a visit to the hospital, given 'all clear', on I went. Heavy, painful bleeding – ignored, on I went. A frozen right shoulder and depression – yay – I left my job, started to Home Ed' my daughter, re-trained, decided to move, found out I had a Uterine Fibroid, started to look inward – each opening, each real, actual change was an awakening, a shift of energy, a healing, all guiding, leading me to and through transformation.

I have found sitting in Circle and connecting with other women to be a most beautiful, potent and deeply healing experience. I joined Jules Heavan's Turtle Lodge and sat in Circle with wild wise women for 5 years. In these Circles I learnt to listen to my inner voice, to hear the wise voice of others. I learnt to Journey, to connect to my Soul wisdom, the stories of my ancestors, meet my shadow selves and how to interpret the symbols, sounds and senses I experienced through the practices, rituals and ceremony's Jules facilitated. I learnt how to listen to my body through poetry and music and silence. How to release hidden, wrapped up, concealed, buried pain using my voice and tears and rage. How to sing balance and peace and love into my womb, how to feel the flow of energy through my body. I learnt how to speak my Truth, to speak words I had not previously dared to speak. I learnt to reclaim and love my sacred feminine self. Vulnerability became my ally, my strength.

I learnt to take off my armour and have a cup of tea!

How might you find the courage to take off your armour?

Who and what would empower you to quest for your healing processes?

Your first step to taking off your armour may be to carve out some space for yourself and dream into what you need and want.

Are You Nurturing and Nourishing Yourself?

When we have the wisdom to know that everything ends and with each ending there is a new beginning, we release ourselves from unproductive, disabling worry, we have learnt to look beyond the obvious. We know that with each new beginning there is an opening to something more, something different. When we have learnt to pay attention to our intuition and instinct, to pay attention to what our child is communicating, we know we have finally learnt to dance with the life, death, life cycle.

With your wisdom you will have chosen your own terms of reference and know it is OK to change your mind. You will know who to choose to share your fears with, and when. You will know which friends and family members 'get it' and that it is OK to ask for their help. You will hone your intuitive and instinctual skills to see or sense those people who are projecting their shadow stuff onto you or your child and you will learn to set clear, healthy boundaries. You will know that nurturing and nourishing yourself, in the ways which suit you, regularly and consistently will keep you physically, spiritually, soulfully and mentally well. You will know when to arrange a party, when to rest, when to go on holiday, when to say no, when to say yes. You will know that there is a new paradigm rising, that with each new awakening, each person stepping into her or his healing, we step nearer to truly healing Mother Earth. You will know that our children, *all* our children will have a beautiful, safe, creative, pleasurable world to live in if we commit now to *staying* awake, *doing* our inner work, *living* a kind, compassionate, connected life.

As I have said on a number of occasions now, there is great power and potency being with other women! We have though been taught to be wary of each other, to be in competition with each other, to distrust each other. My experiences as a girl and young woman were often that and it took a long time for me to feel comfortable in groups of women.

More and more I do now find women who want to talk about their blood, their menopause experiences, their relationship with their child, their fears. They want to *gather their bones* and stand in their authority and Truth. Menstruation and Menopause are not ignored or whispered about in the company I keep. We talk about being a woman freely and enthusiastically, with gentleness, with rage and with compassion for our self and for each other.

I started an online Circle recently, Menopause Wisdom, which I hold each month between my Dark Moon Circles. The conversations we have are open, full of enquiry and shared knowledge and experience.

I learnt many, many years ago when I trained to be an Inclusion Group Facilitator and again more recently when I trained to be a Soulful Facilitator, that setting some agreements for a Women's Circle helps to create a safe and held space.

I always ask at the beginning of the Circles I hold for us to agree; that whatever is shared in Circle stays in Circle. That when a woman speaks, she is uninterrupted, all the other women listen. That we do not make comments about what others have said. That we speak only of our own experience or how what someone else has shared resonates for us. I also encourage everyone to speak in the first person *"I know I feel when…."*, rather than *"You know how you feel when…."*

Being heard is very powerful and deeply healing.

And sometimes, these conversations happen just by sitting around the kitchen table having a cup of tea. Where ever we meet as women, in whatever way, there is always magic!

So, I leave you with a question, why not have a go at creating what works for you and your 'tribe', experiment, have fun and more than anything else, be kind and gentle with yourself dearest wise woman.

A meditation to nourish yourself

I have used guided meditations for many years now as part of my personal practice, in the Circle's I hold and with individual clients. I particularly like creative visualisations, I feel them as ancestral storytelling, which take me on a journey, giving me space and time to relax and go inwards. I have discovered through experimenting with a multitude of practices that what works for me are meditations of walking in nature, dancing, laying down and resting, and Shamanic Journeying (not strictly a meditation I suppose but I love Journeying).

Dark Moon Visualisation

Find a quiet, safe space where you will be undisturbed.

Switch off your phone.

Light a candle and perhaps play some gentle music.

Lay down on the floor or sofa and make sure you are comfortable and warm.

When you feel settled and ready, place your hands over your belly and breathe deeply into your womb centre for several minutes.

As your breath deepens, allow and begin to connect and open to your womb wisdom.

Stay with this connection for several minutes.

Take one final deep breath and as you exhale, allow a sigh or a sound to be released.

Now, breathing to your own pace and rhythm, imagine you are sitting by a gently flowing stream.

Pause

To your side is crackling fire, keeping the night air warm as you gaze into the flames.

Pause

Above you, is a clear, star filled sky.

Pause

Your attention is drawn to the energy from the dark moon, unseen but powerfully present.

You become aware of your womb centre once again,

your centre of creativity,

of nurturing

of nourishment

Pause

While you continue to focus on your womb centre, the moon's energy bathes you in the mystery and magic of darkness

washing over your aura, flowing through your body,

until your womb is filled with the energy of dreams, visioning and rest

Pause

As you lay with the potency of the dark moon energy in your womb centre, notice and allow whatever arises.

Pause

When you are ready, take three deep breaths, exhaling with a sigh or sound.

Wiggle you fingers and toes.

Have a yawn and stretch, open your eyes and smile.

Take a few moments to write in your journal.

A final word on vulnerability. As you now know, I record my dreams as a practice. When I started writing this book, if Molly was in a dream, I *always* interpreted her presence as a symbol of vulnerability, interpreting the vulnerability as her being in danger of harm or hurt.

Now, at the end of writing this book there has been a shift. Molly stills turns up in my dreams, but she currently, is no longer a symbol of the vulnerability I have just described. She is now a symbol of freedom, expression and of being unbound, still vulnerable but from a very different perspective.

As Brené Brown says in her book 'Braving the Wilderness', *"vulnerability is not weakness, it's our most accurate measure of courage".*

She goes on to ask *"Are we willing to create courageous spaces so we can be fully seen?*

I believe Molly does *exactly* that, it is a most precious gift she brings to the world.

I love that this shift has happened for two reasons, one, I have moved away from the strong hold of my fear for Molly after I am gone. Two, I have moved towards perceiving her as a whole person *without* me. I have learnt to honour her ability to exist without me. It is time for me to step away from the fear and know Molly is the bright shining star I have always known her to be, and that it is her light, her love, her laughter and her playfulness which *she* gifts to the world independently of me or anyone else.

When Molly was a very small baby, Rob and I were sitting in a café, the woman at the next table leant over to gaze at Molly. She asked me what my baby's name was.

"Molly Moonbeam Sunrise" I replied.

The woman continued to gaze at Molly and said *"Oh, my goodness, we need more Molly Moonbeams in this world"*

I am deeply grateful for that woman's insight and the beautiful words she spoke. They have remained in my thoughts all these years and when life has felt unbearably difficult, that moment in time has often brought me back to a place of absolute knowing that Molly is a Moonbeam, casting her spell of love into our world.

Acknowledgments

To Rob, for your love, encouragement, faith and support throughout the process of me writing this book and for making it easy for me to share our journey. I am so happy we are walking our paths together, with love.

To Jake, my beautiful son, thank you for your honesty and for talking with me and sharing your thoughts about the 'hard stuff'. I love you to the moon and back!

To Tracy for sitting round the kitchen table with me and listening to pieces as I wrote them. Your response and wisdoms gave me both confidence and excitement about what I was writing.

To all the womb wise women I have sat in Circle with, where together we have laughed, danced, cried and shared infinite wisdoms.

To all Molly's friends and PA's, past and present, you have helped Molly to live her life independently from her family and expand her life experiences. Thank you for your love and your willingness to learn and to value Molly within your life.

To Jules Heavans whose love and guidance has been a constant and empowering bright beautiful light for so many women.

To Nicola Humber who offered me the pathway to becoming an author. I am so grateful for your belief in my book and for showing me the Unbound way of writing.

To my daughter Molly, whose free spirit and love of life has taught me to think outside of the box.

Resources

<u>Organisations</u>

Parents for Inclusion – https://m.facebook.com

Inclusive Solutions – https://inclusive-solutions.com/product/keys-to-inclusion/

Alliance for Inclusive Education – https://allfie.org.uk

Moon Mothers UK – www.wombblessingsuk.com

<u>Books</u>

Incurably Human by Micheline Mason

Women who Run with the Wolves by Clarissa Pinkola Estes

Heal Your Inner Good Girl and Unbound by Nicola Humber

New Menopause Years The Wise Woman Way by Susun S. Weed

Burning Woman by Lucy H Pearce

Wild Power by Alexandra Pope and Sjanie Hugo Wurlitzer

Belonging by Toko-pa Turner

Glossary

Wild - a term used by Clarissa Pinkola Estes in her book Women Who Run With The Wolves – meaning, 'a woman who thunders after injustice, the eyes of intuition, the one we leave home to look for, the one we come home to, she is the life/death/life force…'

Unbound - a term coined by Nicola Humber in her book Unbound, meaning 'a woman living her fullest, freest, most magnificent life'.

The mother wound - wounding created through lack of adequate or good enough mothering. A mother who was not emotionally available to you as a child. The wounding is often a repetition of your mother's own mother wound.

Vulnerability - as defined by Dr Brené Brown, is "uncertainty, risk and emotional exposure." Brené says that "vulnerability is the birthplace of love, belonging, joy, courage, empathy and creativity. I say "Yes to that!"

Gathered my bones - as defined by Clarissa Pinkola Estes in her book Women Who run with The Wolves, meaning a woman who remembers, who has come back to her wild, instinctual self, her wild soul, who does her inner work.

SENCO – Special Educational Needs Co-ordinator. A person in a school setting who has the responsibility of overseeing the 'special educational needs' of individual pupils. Including providing policy making, training, managing staff teams in the area of SEN.

EYDCP - Early Years Development and Childcare Partnership

Pi – Parents for Inclusion

PA – Personal Assistant

DP – Direct Payments